AFFINITY TO AFFLUENCE

Attract Wealth and Live Your Desired Life

AFFINITY TO AFFLUENCE

Attract Wealth and Live Your Desired Life

Gordon
You Amaze me!

To your Desired Life!

[signature]

JEFF RAMSPERGER
Award Winning Author

Foreword by **RAYMOND AARON**
New York Times Best Selling Author

Affinity to Affluence Attract Wealth and Live Your Desired Life
First edition published by Jeff Ramsperger

www.thespeakerscompany.com

Copyright © 2018 Jeff Ramsperger

ISBN: 978-1-77277-221-0

Publisher 10-10-10 Publishing Markham, ON Canada

TABLE OF CONTENTS

DEDICATION

This book is dedicated to my mother and father Madeleine and John Ramsperger, and to my wife Jivanne and daughter Erin.

ACKNOWLEDGEMENT

To my immediate family, Terry, Heather, Julie, Kaeden, Madeleine, Jimmy, Denise, James, Jonathan, Joyce and Gary B.

I would like to thank my clients for the support over many years, I remain eager to serve you.

Friends and influencers who have supported me in writing this book:

Walt R, Wennie R, Glenn F Joan F, Tim Y, Raymond A, Karyn M, Emma A, Barbara P, Colin S, Cheryl I, Kelly L, Lee D, Amit A, Swapna A, Mo H, Misty B, Kula S, Virginia G, Marsha L, Mike S, Heather E, Amy B, Brian P, Jenn L, Ken F, Scott B, Carson A, Barrie Z, Bernd Z, Ian P, Lisa M, Stuart P, Stuart T Lester K, Vince J, Ryan F, Kevin F, Heather F, Craig B, Brian B, Steve W, Steve S, Tony N, Amanda N, Lily L, Michael L, Fernando J, Lindsey M, Rose S, Rosie D, Irene L Amanda S, Eddie B, Brad L, Caroline E, Andrew D, Shabbir A, Brent F, Joe F, Jordan S, Mathew S, Edit C, Dick T and Joel S.

Special thanks to Kim Thompson-Pinder for your amazing editing and guidance.

FOREWORD

Do you want to be wealthy and live the rich lifestyle?

Do you feel this is an impossible dream? Have you ever thought to yourself, "I would be wealthy but..." It is these BUTS that are keeping you in debt, frustrated and living a life that you do not want.

Are you aware that wealth is not as hard to achieve as you may think? I bet that you were taught that the road to wealth is through hardwork, saving every penny and a strong dose of good luck. Or, that you may never become successful. Jeff will help you move past any obstacles to success and prosperity!

How many times have you wanted to quit your job but couldn't because you needed the money? Have you watched others take vacations to exotic places and the best that you can do is a 'staycation'? Do you watch others live their dreams and do what they love, while you are trapped in obligations and responsibilities that leave you unfulfilled? Do you want to move forward but feel like every time you do, you get shoved backwards?

What affect do your subconscious thoughts have on how your life is right now? They come out every time you say BUT... each time you say that, it is your subconscious beliefs trying to give you a 'practical' reason why your dreams may seem impossible.

What if there were a way to conquer those thoughts and make money work for you instead of against you?

Affinity to Affluence by Jeff Ramsperger, looks at money, riches and wealth from all angles including physical, spiritual and practical. He has learned over his many years of success that it is not as hard as you think when you understand the Laws of Money. When you work within these laws, money can't help but come to you. When you break them, money will always be falling through your fingers, never to return.

Jeff also shows you how to take 1 percent and make it equal 100 percent. How can you make one into a hundred? Simple. Think of a boat rudder. By turning it one degree, you will in a short space of time be going in the opposite direction. Jeff teaches you the small changes you need to make, that produce the biggest results in your life. One percent change in each of the areas mentioned in this book, will see a great harvest of wealth, allowing you to live your dreams.

Jeff makes it clear which paths to wealth are the best to take. In a world where there are so many get rich quick schemes and self-proclaimed gurus, Jeff provides a refreshing and balanced look at what it takes to earn money. He gives you choices and then how best to use them. It is about you becoming your true self, finding your passion and being able to become wealthy in the process.

One of the vehicles to wealth creation Jeff focusses on is real estate. Having been involved in over 1100 real estate transactions, I can tell you Jeff knows what he is talking about. There are many different strategies that you can apply and Jeff shares with you the three best to start with. Jeff's real estate experience will educate you on how to invest in real estate and propel you to success.

It takes courage to take those first steps from where you are, to where you want to be. Congratulations! You have made a great first step in reading this book. It will give you a strong foundation upon which to grow and help you overcome major obstacles that you didn't even know existed.

You are on an incredible journey and the best is yet to come! I know that you will look back years from now and be grateful that you decided to read and act on what you have read.

To a Successful Journey to Affluence,

Raymond Aaron
New York Times Bestselling Author

CHAPTER 1:

MY LIFE WAS INCOMPLETE

There is no passion to be found playing small - in settling for a life that is less than the one you are capable of living.

Nelson Mandela

Some people are born to be entrepreneurs, and others do not realize their entrepreneurial gifts until well into adulthood. For me, I had a natural understanding of how to make money from the time I was young, or so I thought ...

My mother loved to tell a story of when I was five or six years old. I would walk down the road and knock on all the neighbours' doors. I would tell them that I would sweep their porch and their walkways for fifty cents.

I would get a retainer of twenty-five cents to start. Then I would offer the kid who lived across the street the twenty-five cents to do the work, and he would sweep all the porches. I would give him the twenty-five cents, and then I would go back and pick up the remainder and make a profit.

The rest of my growing-up years and into my twenties were spent starting and building businesses, and I thought I knew it all and I had nothing left to learn.

EVERYTHING CHANGED

I got involved in a business that was set to flourish. I poured a lot of money, time and sweat equity into it to ensure success. It was going to succeed, but I made a critical mistake and lost almost everything.

That was twenty years ago. I had hit a wall that seemed impregnable. Nothing I had done in the past was going to work to get me out of this mess. On top of that, I was raising a young daughter on my own. She was a baby at the time.

It got so bad that I found myself down to my last nickel with no hope of life changing.

> *It's easy to believe in miracles until you need one!*

That was around the time that faith found me, and I also realized I didn't know everything, it was time for me to learn more. A mentor came into my life, Tim Young, but at the time I didn't know what a mentor was and how he would impact my life. Things didn't improve immediately, but I was able to make it through that time.

We started by studying a book together and then began to work on a course called "Worldview for the Marketplace" that took almost two years to complete. It was an eye opener for me. There were so many things I was doing wrong and still had to learn.

The turning point came during that time. Money was still incredibly tight. I was down to my last ten dollars—that was it. There was very little food in the fridge and I had a little girl to feed. I was in my basement and it was so hard not to give into the fear, but I made a choice. I fell down to my knees with a sincere heart and said, "Thank you," and I meant it. Even though this may seem strange, I knew this was the best thing that had ever happened to me. I was completely humbled. It's amazing what happens when you can be thankful for the hardships and mean it.

Later that day a miracle happened. There was a cheque in my mailbox, from an anonymous sender, for $500. Now $500 isn't a tremendous amount of money, but when you are down to your last $10 and you have no food in the fridge, it counts.

I was overjoyed with that and the fact that it was anonymous. To this day I do not know who sent that cheque.

A NEW DAY

That anonymous cheque changed me from the inside out. I knew, and I knew that I knew, deep down in my heart, that the money and my finances were going to get better. I now had faith and hope on my side.

Within days of that event, I was contacted by an old client of mine. He said, "You know, Jeff, I trust you so much. You did such a good job for me the last time that I have a project for you in Dubai. I want you to come."

It was hard leaving my daughter behind, but I knew she was in good hands and this was just the opportunity I needed to get back on my feet in a short time.

He sent me first-class plane tickets. He put me up in a five-star hotel and there was a limo driver at my beck and call twenty-four hours a day. I worked with his suppliers to solve some problems and renegotiate some prices that had gotten too high.

It was a successful trip. Then the first temptation came. They offered me a full-time position there that would make me a millionaire. Of course, I turned it down.

You are probably thinking to yourself, "You turned it down?" Yes, I did, because there was something way more important to me than money, and that was my daughter. If we had moved there I would have been rich, but my daughter would have paid the price for it with her freedom. I would not let that happen, so I turned the job down.

After that, I was back in the game. My phone started ringing. I was being offered positions and contracts. My life had completely changed. I found an amazing woman, Jivanne, and we got married. We lived in a nice home in a nice neighbourhood. Life became easy. Little did I know that I was being prepared for the next stage of my journey.

THE COMPLACENCY TRAP

When life is good, and the money is coming in, it is easy to get complacent, and that is what I did. We were not wealthy, but we were upper middle class and comfortable.

Even though life was good, I started thinking about the future and what it would look like. I could see middle class was the new poverty. We were seeing a systematic elimination of the middle class. Wages were not going up with inflation, taxes and gas prices. If I didn't make moves now, my end years might not be that good. Some people have golden pensions and they are set. I did not. I had been in business for myself all of my life.

Because I was now ready, the solution landed in my lap. Jivanne and I heard a commercial on the radio for a *Rich Dad, Poor Dad* seminar. We went, and my eyes were opened. I bought the *Rich Dad, Poor Dad* book. I read it from cover to cover. I read it more than once, and it changed my life.

My eyes were opened again! All of a sudden, all the knowledge I had gained when I studied with Tim twenty years ago started coming to the forefront of my mind. My wife and I decided to start getting educated in real estate. We took many courses. We spent quite a bit of money, and we found mentors.

Whenever you want to start a business, one of the best strategies you can adopt is to surround yourself with people who are really good at it. That's what we did.

Our journey is certainly not complete; we are still growing. The difference is that we have stepped off the ladder and we are on the elevator now. We are buying properties, we are working with investors, and my retirement years (although I never intend to truly retire) are on track to be very good financially.

MENTORS MAKE A DIFFERENCE

Some people have told me that you don't need mentors to become successful, and that is true, but a mentor gets you there faster, and you miss most of the pitfalls.

A mentor is like a Sherpa. If you were going to climb Mount Everest and tried to find your own path up that hill, your likelihood of success would be small. But when you get a mentor, someone who has been up that hill before, they can not only take you up the best path, they can ensure your success.

A mentor is someone who in a single sentence can say something so profound it will change your life. I currently have several mentors. Each one makes my journey possible.

Some people have given me the excuse that they can't afford a mentor and then gone to their friends for advice. First of all, a mentor is not your broke friend. Friends and family usually do not offer good advice. They have not done it and, most likely, although unintentionally, they don't want you to succeed, because *they* have no intention of succeeding. They don't want you to leave them.

A mentor doesn't always have to cost money. One of the first steps you can take is to surround yourself with the right people. It's a commonly used phrase: your network is your net worth.

Surround yourself with people who are going in the same direction. Next, you can start volunteering: if someone is doing it exactly right and you want to be part of that, ask them if you can help them. Make yourself available; learn while doing good for someone else. Let them see your worth. Pay your dues.

Take what you learn while volunteering and then apply it to your life. It is a journey; it doesn't matter where you start but where you finish.

MONEY ISN'T JUST PHYSICAL

The accumulation of wealth starts with the spiritual, not the physical, "spiritual" being defined as something that is not physical that you cannot touch. For instance, a thought is a spiritual thing. One of the main spiritual tenets of money is knowledge.

Success very seldom falls into your lap. Sometimes, when you go to seminars, they will say all you have to do is this one simple thing and you will be rich. I'm here to tell you that's crap. It takes action and knowledge plus time. The amount of time can vary, but with the more you know, and the more action taken, you can certainly generate riches with some expediency.

You need to combine the spiritual, which could also be labelled as "mindset," with the physical. You can have a million-dollar mind, but if you don't get off the couch, nothing is going to happen. You need to take action. It is the combination of the spiritual and the physical that will lead to your success. That is one of the main premises of this book.

Knowledge is the key that unlocks the door.

Action occurs when you open the door and step through.

Mentorship allows you to ask for help to have the door opened for you.

In the first half of this book, we are going to look at the spiritual/mindset aspects of money and success. You need to have those in place before you move onto Section 2 of the book, which focuses on the actions you can take to get wealthy. When you combine the two, it gives you a roadmap that you can use to ensure you achieve success in a timely fashion.

This book is a culmination of knowledge and years of experience that I am sharing with you, so you can go further, faster. This book is a system to get you on a proven path to an improved life with financial security.

I invite you to join me on this journey and become the most successful you that you can be. Turn the page and let's get started, shall we?

SECTION 1:

THE TRUTH ABOUT MONEY AND WEALTH

Jeff Ramsperger

CHAPTER 2:

ARE YOU READY TO BE WEALTHY?

Consult not your fears but your hopes and your dreams. Think not about your frustrations, but about your unfulfilled potential. Concern yourself not with what you tried and failed in, but with what it is still possible for you to do.
Pope John XXIII

Not everyone is ready to be wealthy. If they were, we would all be rich! Wealth is something that you earn the right to, and that is what we are going to discuss in this chapter: how to prepare yourself to be wealthy.

There are only two directions you can head in life financially: forward or backward. There is no staying still. As long you continue to make the same amount of money, you will move backward, because the cost of everything keeps going up. Over time, even if you are doing well, the quality of your lifestyle will go down.

THE FIVE HOLLYWOOD SCRIPTS

It is said that in Hollywood, movies tend to be based on five scripts. In our lives it is the same way. There are typically five stories we live our lives by. In these examples, three of them keep you broke, poor, and not living the life you want.

The great thing is that, with the proper knowledge and coinciding actions, you can raise yourself up through the levels and become truly wealthy. Each one is based on an emotional state that affects your spiritual state/mindset. The higher your emotional state, the greater your ability to produce and keep wealth. Let's look at each one and see not only where you are, but how you can rise to the next one.

Trepidation

Starting at the bottom, **trepidation**. Trepidation is one of the lowest forms of emotion you can have. When you are in a state of trepidation you are failing to perceive things around you properly. You have a hard time learning and understanding even the simple lessons of success.

Trepidation is also a state of fear, which is a failure to confront the future. Most fears are not real. They can be warning signs in our lives, but when people make fears a reality and live based on fear, they are unable to function. The person who lives in this state of being is going down fast. They will most likely start to experience health issues. The world is always negative. They perceive negatively, and they let their emotion control their life.

The best way to get out of this stage is to recognize that you are there and make the decision that you are not going to live your life based on fear anymore. That decision to act will help you have the courage to face your fears and conquer them over time.

Weariness

The next level, just slightly up, would be **weariness.** Weariness applies to many people in the middle class. "I can't wait to retire. I am tired of going to work every day." "I come home from work and I am exhausted. I just want to sit and watch TV." Weariness reflects a dissatisfaction with life. People, if you cannot wait to retire, you are probably not living life the way you should be right now. If you are waiting to do everything at the end of your days, it's probably not going to get done.

For example, my friend Kim's father-in-law worked all his life for his retirement, but when it came he spent it in bad health. It continually deteriorated until he died last year. He never got a chance to enjoy what he had worked so hard for.

This emotional state is hard to get out of because people are not dissatisfied enough to do something about it. All they do is complain about their dissatisfaction. This becomes an infinite circle where nothing is changing for the good and life is slanted toward the negative. It's very hard to climb out of this emotional state on your own. It's a kind of apathy. You are not happy with where you are, but you are not willing to do the things you need to do to get out. It usually takes a significant event to bring someone out of this. In rare cases, they make the decision themselves.

If this is you, don't wait for something major to happen in your life to make the decision to move forward as you want. Start now. Make some small changes and, as you see results, you will want more.

Reactionaryism

The third level, which is where the majority of the population, is **reactionaryism.** This is a resistance to change. Life can be pleasant in this state of being. You have a decent job. You get to go on vacations. You have some money and you are financially stable—probably too stable, because instead of making changes in your life you wait to react to the things that happen.

You have become complacent and aren't seeing the potential perils coming your way. Instead of making sure that fires don't ruin your life, you wait for them to ignite and then panic trying to put them out. You then get complacent again and wait for the next fire to happen. Eventually you spend a lot of time putting out fires and don't enjoy life anymore.

Your life is slowly slipping away with an unawareness of its direction.

For example, you don't spend the time that you could with your parents, and only when they either become too sick for you to enjoy them or they die do you really appreciate what you had.

You sort of take care of your health until something drastic happens, like a heart attack or you get diagnosed with diabetes. Then all of sudden you are doing everything you can to stay alive.

You don't take control of your finances and keep using credit to buy the things you want, until one day you realize you can no longer afford the payments and all those things you used to enjoy become a constant reminder of the heavy weight you carry.

The best things to focus on at this stage are awareness and action. Do not become complacent. Know what is going on in your life, and make conscious choices to keep life moving forward, not backward.

Discrimination

The fourth level is to be **discriminating.** This is where life begins to soar. Being discriminating is having the ability to appreciate the small things, having the ability to see the good in things that others would see differently or view as negative. The discriminating person sees problems as opportunities for power, for change. The discriminating person is also very analytical; they avoid 'group think,' which is rampant in today's society.

A discriminating person doesn't hear commentary on a news channel and then decide that is *their* commentary. A discriminating person will take that information and analyze it to see both sides and find out what their truth is. A discriminating person has the analytical ability to look at a business deal in a different way and find out the best way to position it. Not only for themselves, but to make it a good position for the other party in the deal as well.

Those who discriminate love life. The negative filter that is in the last three ways of being is barely noticeable at this level. Good things just seem to happen. It doesn't mean they are never going to have a health issue or anything like that. But, typically, when your mind is healthy, your whole being is healthy. The people around you are healthy. Your relationships are more meaningful and healthier. People look forward to seeing you, because you bring them up and you make better financial decisions.

You are the opposite of reactionary: you are more aggressive about creating and being change. You do it for the love of it. Because you appreciate the little milestones. You are thankful for the things you have in your life.

Blessedness

The fifth level, to live life in is the state of **blessedness** which is truly rare, but possible.

A person at this level has favour in their life. This is a person who sees only beauty in the world. Who really cares for other people. This person usually has incredible wealth. Not that wealth makes you blessed, but wealth is not only financial—it can be in your relationships as well. The blessed person would say, "Wow, I haven't heard from George in a long time," and then their phone rings. Or, "I wonder what it would be like to do that someday?" and then the opportunity comes within days.

Everybody has experienced this way at some point in their life. The purpose of this exercise and my teaching the five scripts, levels, is to change your life. When you wake up everyday and are truly thankful for the things in your life – the good, the bad and the challenging – your life will change. When you have an appreciation for life and become analytical like the discriminating person, your live will reach a new level. You will filter things and lead a blessed life.

This is not an easy level to follow. Most of the people we surround ourselves with are somewhere in the first three, and most likely in the second two—weariness and reactionaryism. But the more we can surround ourselves with people who are discriminating, and even blessed, the more rapidly our mind will adjust to living a blessed life and the more rapidly things will come to us.

We are not necessarily in control of everything. But our mind is such a powerful tool, our thoughts and vibration from our being not only affects circumstances around us but can have an effect around the world.

YOUR COMFORT ZONE WILL BE STRETCHED

You can't stay the way you are and move up levels in life. You must change, and that requires your comfort zone to be stretched to accept the new growth.

The elements of fear and the weaknesses in your life don't want you to change, because as you grow they die. These emotions fight you, make you uncomfortable, and give you this sense of dread that something bad will happen if you try to move forward.

The best way to get over fear is through knowledge, because knowledge is power.

Fear is an emotional state; it is not a stop sign. Fear can be good. Fear of falling off a high building is a good thing. But it doesn't mean you can't stand at the edge.

You can combat weakness. "I don't want to do that because I am weak; I am not good at it." Education helps you be more confident. Weaknesses can all be overcome, but knowledge is the key. The fact that you are reading a book like this means you are ready to get uncomfortable and getting uncomfortable can create some of the greatest successes in your life.

I had a realization that really rattled my comfort zone and changed my life. It was twenty years ago. I realized that the education system teaches you only to become a good employee, not a good entrepreneur. If I was going to become an amazing entrepreneur, I was going to have to change what I was learning.

When I started gaining knowledge about different things that had a much larger world view, I saw the world in a much different way. All of a sudden, the things that seemed inconceivable or seemed impossible seemed entirely possible and a lot easier to get to than what my previous education, from our public schools and colleges and universities, had taught me.

For instance, in real estate I was amazed to find out that it's actually about a Grade 5 level math that is required. If you learn how to analyze the numbers in a certain way, you can take an investment property that might get a 1 to 3 percent return and get 20 to 30 percent on it. All it requires is a slightly different way of thinking about things.

When I started to make that simple concept real, I started thinking about other areas in my life. I started thinking about my business. How can these very basic concepts change my business? It's not super advanced quantum-physics knowledge that is required. It's just being able to look at things, examine them for what they are, and then walk around to the other side of the table and look at them from a different angle. Then walk back to the first side of the table and look at them again. Try to understand both points of view.

It's amazing how, when we remove those filters that are so engrained in our life, things become alive.

Things that seem complicated become very realistic, and when it becomes realistic it becomes your new reality.

WEALTH ISN'T WHAT YOU THINK IT IS

To most people, being wealthy is just something unattainable. It's the other guy—it's that snobby woman with the Rolls Royce. It's that guy I could never hang around with because I've never actually given it a chance. A wealthy person is someone that a lot of people judge falsely based on 'evidence' they have gathered from other people's opinions to create their own—they've engaged in group think.

Wealth can be an accumulation of money, certainly, but being wealthy in relationships is significant as well. I believe that a truly wealthy person is wealthy in both finances and relationships.

Wealthy people have the ability to make great changes in their circumstances and do things that are unachievable for other people because, unlike others, they don't let their lack hold them back.

I am sure we can agree that having wealth is better than not having wealth. So, why is there a stigma attached to it? Why are so many people trapped in being reactionary about their life rather than pursuing wealth? When you stop to think about it, it's astounding.

The problem is that most people are in reactionaryism, so they are not thinking about it. If you start thinking about it, you become more about causing change then reacting to it. If we can agree that wealth is a good thing, it's just what you do with it that makes a difference, why not walk toward being wealthy?

DOES PASSION PLAY A ROLE IN WEALTH?

One of my mentors taught me that procrastination is a gift in my life. Now, procrastination is something I have excelled at over the years, so I was excited to learn how that was going to work.

Procrastination is your spirit's way of telling you what you should do and what you should not do, what you're passionate about and what you are not passionate about. When you discover that the things you are not passionate about are the things you procrastinate over, life becomes different. They could be the easiest things to do, but they become impossible because you were never meant to do them. On the other hand, you may take on incredibly challenging tasks and flourish at them because they are your passion.

Now, let's look at this with a dose of reality. Let's say you make $20 an hour, or $30 an hour, or even $40/$50 an hour—whatever the level of your income—and you take that hourly rate and then look at the things you have been procrastinating about. Perhaps it's detailing the inside of your car. Ask, "Can I get someone to clean the inside of my car for less money per hour than what I make?"

If the answer is yes, this is probably something you should not be doing. When you follow your passions and find out how they can be turned into wealth, wealth becomes a lot more achievable.

DO WEALTHY PEOPLE THINK DIFFERENTLY FROM THE AVERAGE PERSON?

When you are rich or wealthy, in both relationship and finances you most likely act according to a different point of view than someone who just reacts to life.

Your mind has the ability to control the amount of money you have and the depth of your relationships. Having an understanding that it starts in the mind and it starts in knowledge, wealthy people process things through different filters. Typically, a wealthy person does not see a lofty goal as reaching for the unattainable. They see it as a problem that needs to be solved.

A wealthy person can look at the scale of a project that's way beyond their means differently from the way someone who is not wealthy looks at it—buying a first investment property, for example. It's the same scale, but a wealthy person sees it as a problem that needs to be overcome. The problem is not overwhelming. It's a fun problem to solve.

If someone is coming from a place of lack, they let their circumstances control them. "I can't do that, because I'm not as good as that person. That person obviously has something special," or "It must be nice that that person was born into wealth and has a better education than I do."

Well, the fact is, most self-made wealthy people don't come from an advanced educational background. They learned at the school of life. They changed how they think or have an ability to think in a different way.

Once you can start to process things in that different way, in that way of looking at life through beauty and wanting to lead that blessed life and processing through those filters, you can go forward, and the problems seem a lot smaller. You can break them into smaller components. You don't necessarily have to let your circumstances hold you back. It is possible to buy a property with no money down. It is possible to make money in business without even having the business set up yet.

One of the proud-father moments I've had recently was when my daughter decided to start a new business and she called me, knowing firmly who her father is: a father with a vast interest in business and running businesses. She anticipated everything I was going to say, including, "How much in sales do you already have?" When she told me the amount, I was impressed! Then she said, "Now I'm going to solve the problem of getting the product."

This isn't something she was an expert at. She had a good idea; she just didn't have the business yet. She already knows how to fulfil it, and she knows the steps to make this come true, but she's learned from the things that I have taught her, and she really, really made me proud that day. Now she's got more customers and she has fulfilled her first contracts. She's got another viable part-time business, that could become full-time.

So clearly, she got out of her comfort zone. Most people concern themselves with ideas like, "Well, I can't have a business until I develop a logo." A logo is probably the last thing you need to think about. If you want to find out if you have a business or not, see if you can get sales. Your customers will tell you if it's a good business or not. You might think it's the best business in the world, you might have thought there is the greatest need for it—but if no one is willing to pay you for it, it's not a good business. Don't worry about the logos and all of these other things that prevent you from starting. Get out of your comfort zone and just do it. Take action. Take that small step. Go and make a sale.

KNOW YOUR WHY

If you truly want to be successful, you need to know your why, and not just on a surface level. It must be something deep inside of you. It is only then that you will be able to overcome any obstacle.

Here is a great exercise you can do. I want you to answer these seven questions. Don't answer them quickly. Think them through. Be honest. The truth always sets you free.

What is most important to you?

If you think for too long you will come to the obvious answers. Of course, it is right to say, "Family, God and well-being." All of these are correct answers, but what is truly important to you? What brings you joy? What brings you satisfaction? What needs to be

23

accomplished in your life for you to be truly satisfied? These are all things you must ask yourself when answering the above question.

There are no wrong answers. Do not worry about putting them in order; the priority of the things you will list has no bearing on the exercise. This should take you only a couple minutes, and the first things that pop into your mind are probably the most truthful answers. Now grab a pen and paper, reflect on this question and write your answers.

What are your strengths?

This is a list of your strongest skill sets. Please do not be too specific. For example, you may have a mathematical or artistic mind. You may have the ability to build or, perhaps, to solve problems.

What would you like your tombstone to say?

Again, this is a written exercise. The answer should be clear and concise. Do you want it to say, "Loving parent, built a business, philanthropist?"

What are your deepest passions?

This should be a small list. What is it in you that sparks a fire? Perhaps another way to look at this question is, "What pushes your buttons?" Personally, as an example, I am passionate about my family, music and helping others. I am also passionate (my buttons are pushed) when I see government waste, which means passing on massive debt to our children and grandchildren.

Where can you make the greatest difference?

Please do not think small for this question. Putting together all of the above questions, what direction is it pointing you? Where can you add the most value? Don't worry about how you will get there; this will be discovered a bit later in your journey.

What is holding you back?

When answering this question, you will be temped to say things like lack of money, not enough time or not sure how. Here is how you need to answer this question!

You cannot use an excuse, and you cannot justify.

Instead, this is a test in deep personal honesty. Is it a fear or a weakness, a lack of knowledge? This is for you! An honest assessment will provide your starting point. You will be amazed at how you will overcome it.

ONE LAST THING

One of the greatest realizations I have had was when I went on a transformational retreat. The teaching was fantastic, but it was the people who were at the retreat who gave me one of the best lessons.

It was one of the first times in my life I was surrounded by people who were ultimately positive in their outlook. People who wanted to do great things in their lives. People who were making changes in the larger world. There were people at this retreat who were literally defining what goes on in countries, and they wanted to help me! Really wealthy people are really friendly. Wealthy people want to help you succeed.

As they shared their knowledge with me, it made me realize I needed to expand my vision to include helping others. That is one of the main reasons you are holding this book in your hand. It is now my turn to share my knowledge with you, and I hope you are ready to receive it.

In the next chapter we are going to break down a lot of your barriers. By the end you will be on a higher level. You will be ready for success; you will have set the bricks and mortar of your foundation and be ready to accelerate and grow fast. So, go grab that cup of coffee, take that quick walk around the block, get yourself ready and dive right in.

CHAPTER 3:

WHAT IS MONEY?

Money is an excellent slave, but a terrible master.
P.T Barnum

What is money? So far in this book the words "money," "rich" and "wealth" have all been used. Almost everyone says they want to be rich or they want to be wealthy, but most people don't really know what those terms mean.

It is obvious that you can be rich and wealthy in your relationships, but for the point of these definitions I am going to stick to the monetary factors.

Money is an exchange. Over 90 percent of the population lives in this category: just making money and exchanging it. Rich in Canada means a household income of over $350,000 a year. In the USA it's anything over $250,000 a year. A rich person typically will have material holdings; money is working for them, adding up.

Wealth is meant to be generational, to bless future generations. It includes valuable holdings. It multiplies and typically comes from many sources.

THE SPIRIT OF MONEY

As we tackle the topic of the spirit of money, it is important to note that this is not a religious chapter, although I have faith, and you may or may not have faith. The concepts hold true no matter. If you do have faith and it is a different faith from mine, none of this information should be contradictory to what you know and believe.

Understand this next teaching, it is important to note that there are two systems operating in parallel in this world, the spiritual and the physical. We are spirits placed in physical bodies. There is a life source inside of us that is untouchable. That is spirit.

When talking of things of the spirit and the physical, I will interchange some words. For instance, to represent spirit, depending upon the context I might say "God", "spirit", or "universe." I will refer to the physical as "the world system" or "the physical dimension

This also applies to laws. There are spiritual laws and there are physical laws. There are two systems operating in parallel, the spiritual and the physical.

If you ask someone what a physical law is, the most typical answer you will get is "gravity." There are physical limitations due to gravity. If I walk off the top of a tall building I am going to fall downward, never upward.

There are also spiritual laws. When you ask people if they know of any spiritual laws, some might start reciting the Ten Commandments or some other religious writing.

It's also crucial to note that for the purposes of this chapter, money is physical. You can hold money in your hand. But money is also spiritual.

THE HISTORY OF MONEY

In the earliest days of recorded history, wealth was spirit- or God-given. Wealth was given in five different forms. It was given in land, houses, livestock, gold and silver.

In relating to today's terms, you might consider this: land and houses still are land and houses.

Livestock can also be livestock, but you might also consider this to be employees or a replenishable resource. For example, one employee retires, and you can hire another employee and make money off them. That's a replenishable resource.

Gold would be your assets and your true wealth. Silver would be your cash on hand.

Originally, wealth was given to those whom the spirit trusted and those who were the best managers. This system of operating in wealth went on for many thousands of years.

But then something happened. Mankind created currency and the rules changed. With currency, the world had a system to create and distribute wealth.

This is when a new spirit came upon money, working in parallel with the existing spirit. There has always been good and evil in this world. Mankind is inherently flawed. We can choose to be good or evil.

Mankind had this system born, and he even put his face on it. When that happened, a new spirit came upon money, and it even has a name. Its name is Mammon and it is even listed in the dictionary. The definition of Mammon is wealth personified or deified. Mammon always wants two things.

Number one, Mammon wants to be worshipped. For the love of money is the root of all evil. A person driven by greed has the love of money. For example, an assassin is someone who has no regard for human life and is willing to take someone's life in exchange for money. That is someone who worships Mammon.

The second thing Mammon wants is for you to be its slave. For the borrower is slave to the lender. This is most people. This is how our economy is based. We have an economy based on a debt society.

Most of the population just adds and subtracts. Working in the physical laws, they are slaves to money. For instance, out of paycheques come debts and obligations to be paid. You hope there is enough left after to live on.

But to get riches and wealth, you must work in multiplication and division, which are spiritual laws. This is a big topic and requires many steps. I will be unpacking these steps as you continue through this book. This chapter is to give you an introduction to it.

One thing to remember: money is never to be loved. It is only a tool you use to achieve true wealth.

THE FIVE ACTION STEPS

The original spirit, creator, or God is still in charge of money. Rather than worshipping or being a slave to Mammon, you can find ways to operate within the good spirit of money. One of the ways to break the evil spirit of money is to follow a system.

Action Step 1: Close your circle. Closing the circle means creating a budget. Now, I know this sounds terribly boring, but there is spiritual power in closing your circle. If you would like to have the powerful spreadsheet I use, go to www.affinitytoaffluence.com

When you close your circle, you know how much is enough. Know what you need and plan for what you want. This is a very simple lesson, and yet most people do not follow it. Let's say you are making an income of $70,000. You have a decent car in the driveway, you live in a decent house.

All of a sudden, you get a big promotion and earn $100,000 a year. Most people will go out and buy a new car or a boat, or plan to move. The question is, do you really need to do that?

Know what you need. What you need are the necessities of life. This is not saying that you cannot go out and purchase the luxuries of life, but plan for them first. It would be good if you live in your dream house, but it's not the first thing you do.

Get your money working for you first. Going back to my example, you create a budget. You find out what you actually need, and in your needs assessment you should include things like holidays. That's important. You should include things for family. You should include basic expenditures for entertainment, but you should also have an excess fund. Most people are swimming in debt and can't meet their basic needs, let alone have excess. That means you are not living right and you need to cut back.

Let's assume you are fairly responsible, and you find out your household budget requirement and that you have an excess. Where should your excess funds go? Let's look at the three verticals.

Vertical number one: put aside funds for a rainy day. There will be emergencies. The car or the washing machine will break down. A family member might get sick and you might need to travel within a few hours. You never know when something might happen that requires funds immediately. You should always have a fund for a rainy day.

Vertical number two: make <u>educated</u> investments. I underline the word "educated." This is where your money will work for you. Just a quick note: you can have too much money in your rainy-day fund as well. That is when you should start adding more to your investments. You have to determine what your rainy-day fund should be.

The third vertical: plan to give. There are spiritual laws concerning giving that I get into in depth in my seminars, but here is one to get you started: give, and it will be given to you. In other words, givers gain! It is important to truly understand the principle of giving. When giving, you must never be expecting a return or the spirit will nullify the action. Be a joyful giver!

Action Step 2: Be thankful. This is one of the most important points in the book. This is a really foundational mindset that can set you free, breaking the spiritual bonds of Mammon, and actually putting you in a place, spiritually, where you are ready to receive—not only in the spiritual sense, but in the physical as well.

You need to be thankful for what you have. Concentrate on what you have and not what you lack. Realize what is truly important to you and love it. Gratitude opens the windows of opportunity and starts to direct your life toward your passions. Be slow to complain and quick to compliment. Be the discriminating person who admires the beauty in their surroundings, in other people, globally and beyond. Appreciation and thankfulness really break through spiritual and physical barriers.

Action Step 3: Dare to dream. To dream or to have a vision is to plan your destination. You cannot dream too big. If your dream does not seem outrageous, you are not dreaming big enough. If it appears to be impossible or unattainable, you are on the right track. When dreaming big, incorporate your unique abilities and passions. I suggest that your dreams should be playful.

Understand your why and your reason to succeed. This is one of the key mechanisms that will help your dreams to come true. Write down your dream, post it in a visible place, ask the universe for it three times a day: morning, noon and night. As you do this, be prepared to receive, and count it as reality that has simply not yet been made manifest.

Communicate the desires and dreams of your heart. This is a big key. Communicate with the spirit and communicate with other people who support you and want to succeed themselves. Do not communicate with anyone who will not support you 100-percent. Sometimes it's your spouse, a family member, a best friend. They do not truly support you, and they will try to strip your dreams. They don't mean to do it; it's just a natural reaction when people are living in conservatism or below. They do not want other people to get ahead. They are not being mean to you; it's just where they are.

Include generosity in your dreams. Help others make their dreams come true. Make sure your dream aligns with the good spirit of money. Visualize constantly and be creative!

Action Step 4: Have a belief mindset. Believe and have faith in something bigger than you. If you do not have faith, you really do not have hope. I am not trying to convince you to have any particular faith, but it is my personal opinion that it is important to have faith. If you believe in the Big Bang theory, for instance, it takes a lot more faith to believe that theory than it does to actually have faith in God/the universe.

For example, as I am writing this, I look at my cell phone. My cell phone is a wonder of amazing components. This powerful computer and communication tool is right in my hand. Now, if I were going to compare a cell phone to the Big Bang theory, it would look like this: There is a big explosion in the desert that comes from nowhere. A gale of wind blows, some dust surrounds me, and suddenly my cell phone appears. A cell phone is simplistic compared to a human, this world, the eco system, etc. It takes a lot of faith to believe that. Isn't it much easier to believe in something or someone much bigger than you?

I would also say that if you do not have a faith, or even if you do have a faith and it's not a strong faith, don't overcomplicate it. It's just easier to have faith and make the decision and get it over with. If you try to figure out who created God and things like that ... we don't have enough knowledge to come up with the answers. You will never get them, so don't even think about it.

Faith by definition simply means belief in things yet unseen.

Action Step 5: Attract ethical money. Embrace opportunities. Always be on the lookout. If you see a problem, there's most likely an opportunity there. Embrace problems, embrace opportunities. Be a producer, not a consumer. Create solutions, provide for wants and/or needs. Deliver value first, get compensated second and—this is really important to attract ethical money—love what you do. In Chapter 5 and beyond I expand on this action step in great detail. Do not skip ahead. This book has been written in a systematic format for a reason.

SPIRITUAL AGREEMENT AND CONFIDENCE

As mentioned earlier in this chapter, money is both spiritual and physical. But when someone else gives you money, there is a physical transaction. When they actually hand you money or send you money digitally, that's the physical component.

But, first, before a physical transaction takes place, a spiritual transaction must occur. What do I mean by that? Well, money is a couple of different things in the spirit world. It is agreement, and it is confidence. This is the way our economy works. Our government spends, and the less they have the ability to repay the debt, the value of the dollar goes down. Much like when you need to borrow from the bank and have too much debt: the bank does not have confidence in you to repay the loan, so they won't give you money.

On the other hand, if you don't need money and you go to the bank, they are more than willing to give you money, and on the best terms possible, because they have confidence in your ability to repay.

The second part is the agreement. Although we have physical representations of money—it comes in the form of coins, bills, digital numbers in a bank account—there is always agreement. An agreement can also be in the form of, let's say, a note. I agree to pay you $100 for detailing my car. When you detail my car, you have trust in me, the confidence that our agreement will hold, and I will give you $100. That contract, a purchase order—all these things are agreements.

If you want more money, you need to get more agreement with other people or institutions or businesses, and they must have confidence in you.

When you create lots of confidence, it allows you to close your circle, because you will have more than enough money for your needs, wants and investments.

When you have your own household or business finances under control, and you are a better manager of the resources that have been entrusted to you, more confidence will come, more agreement will come, and you will be ready to receive more money, riches or wealth.

The other part of agreement and confidence is what I would call **cause and effect,** or action and reaction. If you want to make a difference in this world, are you taking action or are you reacting?

If you are at **cause**, you are taking action, you are causing things to happen. You are more likely to get a result than reacting or being at **effect** of your circumstances

We are called to work. We are called to make a difference in this world. We are called to have purpose in this world and manage these resources. If you want more resources to manage, you need to keep your own resources managed.

RELATIONSHIPS — YOUR TRUE NET WORTH

In all of this talk of money, riches and wealth, how to attract more money, how to get more money, and how to be a good steward of money, it needs to be said that your relationships are worth far more than money.

Many times, your relationships will bring you money. It has been said by many, many people that your network is your net worth. That's why your

relationships are so important. Have you ever heard of a billionaire lying on his deathbed, the kind who worshipped Mammon all his life, saying, "I wish I had worked harder"? His greed cost him the thing that, at the end, he realized was most important: relationships; at the end no one was there. There was no one to take that money. There was no one visiting, because there were no relationships.

On the other side we have the billionaire who was giving throughout her life and was just; she always did right by people and had good intent toward everyone. She was able to make money, but she had these key relationships. The outpouring of sympathy for someone like that who is on their deathbed, the tears that go around the world for people like this—that illustrates an accomplished life.

By the way, it should be said that even if you are middle class, lower class or even poor, if you have key relationships you can have a really good life. Money is not the be-all and end-all. Relationships are more important.

For example, look at Mother Theresa. She made the choice not to have money, but the bounty of her relationships with not only her people but her faith and her relationship with God far exceeded any monetary reward. At the end of her life she was mourned worldwide by both rich and poor because of the massive contribution she had made to this world.

THE ETHICS OF WEALTH

Let's finish this chapter strong by bringing everything back full circle to the spirit of money. If you worship Mammon, you can achieve a lot of wealth. Many people in this world have, and they would sell their soul for more riches.

Those people can be rewarded with wealth. But going back to that assassin example from earlier in this chapter: I would venture to say you that someone who is willing to trade human life or to do anything, harming anybody in their way for the pursuit of money, would have a lot of money but their quality of life would be terrible.

It's much better to operate with strong ethics and attract money not from Mammon but from the original

Giver. The one who tells your employer to hire you. The one who provides all of your needs.

Can you see why faith is so important?

The ethics of wealth attract the right spirit and the right money. People feel good about giving you money because they have the agreement and confidence that their money will be well spent and will yield a good return.

This is the side that I hope anyone who reads this book will end up on. The stronger your ethics, the more agreement and confidence other people will have in you.

I would also say it's very hard to have a high standard of ethics if you are being **at effect** or reactionary in life. You must be a doer. Action leads to results.

I am very excited for the next chapter. It is the one I have been waiting to share. I am going to show you how to get the advanced law of attraction to work in your life. I am going to reveal some secrets that few people know and even fewer master. If you can conquer this, watch out—your life is going to change!

Jeff Ramsperger

CHAPTER 4:

THE ADVANCED LAW OF ATTRACTION, PART 1 – THE BASICS

The law of attraction states that whatever you focus on, think about, read about, and talk about intensely, you're going to attract more of into your life.

Jack Canfield

There is so much I want to teach you about the advanced law of attraction that it needs to be divided into two chapters. This is the key that is going to unlock so many doors for you, so I encourage you to read these next two chapters, and reread them until they are planted deeply in your heart. Everything has been leading up to these chapters, and everything afterward depends on you understanding this. I can't stress enough how important the law of attraction is. It will change your life!

The advanced law of attraction is your subconscious mind communicating with other connected beings, as we are all connected by the life force inside us. You can alter or rearrange events by your thoughts.

For example, have you ever thought of a long-lost friend? Perhaps you haven't spoken to or seen this person in years. Right after they've come to mind, they either appear in person or your phone rings and it's this person.

That's the advanced law of attraction in action. Here is another example. Have you ever gone to a busy mall and thought, "Wow, it is packed here, but I know I will get a good parking spot." As you drive close to the entrance, someone backs out, and there is a parking space for you. Your belief made it possible.

This is not mind control. However, the more you control your mind, the more effective you are at attracting things into your life.

IT'S A SPIRITUAL LAW

The advanced law of attraction is a spiritual law that affects the physical world all the time. It is based on your thoughts, which are spiritual things. Some people have been taught a false name-it-and-claim-it philosophy, where you just say something out loud a few times and it comes to you. That is not how laws work.

There are two sides to any law, whether it be physical or spiritual. The first is the good side. Laws protect you and allow you to live a life of freedom and prosperity if you follow them. If you don't, the bad side of the law comes through and you reap the consequences of your bad decisions. The advanced law of attraction is no different. Let's look at both sides.

The Bad Side

You cannot be divided. Either the law works for you or against you; you can't have both at the same time.

You can't have fear and weaknesses in your life and expect good things to happen. Everybody has fears and everybody has weaknesses, but it is the extent to which we let them control our lives that they have power to prevent us from effectively utilizing the advanced law of attraction. You also have to remember Mammon, whom we discussed in a previous chapter. They all work together.

Let's look at fears.

There is **fear of death.** Many people are afraid to die. Death is something we shouldn't fear. Perhaps we don't desire it, but it's inevitable. It's a part of our being. If you have faith, the fear of death really doesn't have a grip on you, because you believe there is hope beyond your body. Fear of death can hold people back from doing all kinds of great, adventurous things. Doing new things constantly helps you become more alive.

For instance, someone might not try hang-gliding because of a fear of death. I don't know what the statistics are, but hang-gliding is done in a safe and controlled environment. It's the same with bungee jumping or learning to drive a race car on a track. These things can bring you to life, get your adrenaline going, make you feel like you are living, but the fear of death holds many people back from having these amazing experiences.

Another is the **fear of poverty.** "Oh, if I invest I might lose." Well, there's always risk if you invest, but there's more risk if you don't invest. I know many people who have been gainfully employed and done well in life, but they never really got ahead because they were scared to take any risk. The fear of poverty is very common in the emotional state called Reactionaryism that was discussed in Chapter 2.

There is also the **fear of criticism.** "What if I fail at doing this? What will people say?" It is better to have failed many times than to have never succeeded. If you play life too safe, you will never get anywhere.

Fear of criticism is powerful in its ability to hold most of the population back. We care way too much about what other people think of us. I love this quote from Eleanor Roosevelt:

"You wouldn't worry so much about what others think of you, if you realized how seldom they do."

One of the other major fears is **fear of ill health.** People with an ailment of some kind might not want to travel because, "What if something happens and I am away from my medical coverage?" There are all kinds of examples of how the fear of ill health will hold you back. I would suggest that, sometimes, it is quite legitimate; however, if it holds you back from living and having great experiences, chances are your health will not improve as a result. In fact, it will most likely deteriorate.

Fear of loss of love is something else that holds people back. It really prevents their minds from expanding, conceiving, dreaming and attracting great things into their lives. You may not be willing to step out of your comfort zone; the fear of criticism or failure may cause you to think that someone you love will think less of you and stop loving you.

There is also a **fear of old age.** "I am too old to do this now. If I had done it twenty years ago, it would have been great. But I am too old now." You are never too old. Get past this fear. Age will place some restrictions in your life, and that is a reality. I suggest to you that once you choose to stop living life to your best capacity, you will be attracting more old-age ailments. Remember your thoughts and being direct what comes in and out of your life.

Again, fears are not based on reality. They can be a warning signal if you are standing on an edge of a tall building looking down, or something like that, but they don't mean you can't go to the edge.

The other thing that holds us back is our weaknesses. Much like fears, weaknesses can be overcome.

Weaknesses include **pride**. It is said that pride comes before a fall. If you even just look at the word "pride," what is the middle letter? It is "I." Pride is really saying "I," or "me," all the time and includes being boastful about yourself.

Now, it's easy to mix up pride and confidence.

Someone who is confident should remain confident. Confidence is what helps you get the agreement and helps bring money into your life. But if you are prideful and a boaster, and you look down on other people as compared to yourself, this is definitely a weakness. People celebrate when a prideful person falls.

Lust is also a huge weakness, particularly in western civilization, where there is access to a great deal of unlawful carnal knowledge. I think men probably are more subject to this than women, although women certainly are not excluded.

A person filled with lust (and this is not to be confused with the emotion of being attracted to your chosen spouse, where a degree of lust is good) has a divided mind. You're wanting the things you lack. You're wanting things that are not rightfully yours. You are dividing your mind and you are losing your effectiveness. A divided mind is simply weak!

Greed is also a weakness. As discussed previously, greed is one of the characteristics that Mammon wants to hold over you. If you are suffering from this, this barrier will prevent you from hitting financial or life goals. As I said earlier, if you sell out to greed you may reap financial reward, but beware of the price you pay. Greed and lust are strongly related. If these take a negative hold in your life, it may be like standing next to a well but with a thirst that is never satisfied.

Slothfulness, or laziness, is an obvious weakness. We talked about taking action in the previous chapter. If you are slothful, you are not taking action. If you do not take any action, nothing is going to happen.

It's nice to want to use the advanced law of attraction to bring good things to you. But part of the way the advanced law of attraction works is that you create what you want in your mind, or you visualize it, *and then you start walking toward it.*

Slothfulness is the opposite of that.

Another weakness is **wrath.** This is a very serious one, one that has personal consequences for you. It is said that forgiveness is not for the other person; it is for you. It releases you from those feelings and lets you out of a type of prison. When you are angry or vengeful toward someone, you just want to get that person back for what they did wrong to you. What you are creating in the spiritual world (for lack of a better word) is a curse upon yourself.

If you hold something against someone and you fantasize about bad things happening to them—well, that's what you will attract into your life. If someone has done an injustice to you, let the universe or God deal with them. You only have to worry about yourself; get rid of that weakness.

Envy is another weakness and is closely related to lust. It's wanting what you don't have. Wanting what someone else has is like saying, "They don't deserve it; I deserve it." This is a wrong emotion. It prevents you from getting what you want.

Each and every one of these fears and weaknesses can be overcome simply by addressing them with truth and knowledge. All of these things, including knowledge, work in your subconscious mind, which communicates these things and can create reality. We are told to visualize the things we want, and again this is just another way of utilizing the power of the advanced law of attraction.

We've mentioned that a lot of things hold you back—Mammon, fears and weaknesses—and that knowledge is the way to overcome this. But remember, this is spiritual. Our battle is not necessarily in the realm of flesh and blood. The first way to overcome what holds you back, now that you have the knowledge, is to start protecting yourself.

One of the best ways to do this is to stop feeding it. Stop surrounding yourself with people who feed these fears. Stop surrounding yourself with slothful people, with envious people, with angry people. Remember, garbage into you is garbage out of you.

If you want to be a high-performance person, you need to put in high-performance fuel. Knowledge is your high-performance fuel. Stay away from the things that have a negative influence on you.

Steep Gradient Statement

Here is the shortcut to addressing your fears and weaknesses with knowledge. Learning is not always as it seems. One of the best ways to gain knowledge is to remove the false realities that reinforce the fears and weaknesses plaguing you.

Most of your fears and weaknesses have been planted in you by other people and past events. Because of these things, you always react to situations based on the emotional or fearful data that resides in your subconscious. You can read a ton of books and attend many seminars, but it is actually removing these things by using fact and truth that will allow wisdom and knowledge to flow and expand.

The Good Side

When you operate on this side of the law, you cannot stop the good from coming to you. Let's look at the things you should fill your mind and your thoughts with.

The first one is **love**. Love conquers all things. Love can do no wrong. God is described as love.

When you love someone, and your heart gets broken, you might think *There is a negative consequence of love.* I have heard people say, "I can never love again. It hurts too much." Well, this is precisely the wrong attitude. Love does conquer all things. The way to overcome a hurt is to love again.

Of course, love brings **joy**. There is no law against joy. We are meant to have joy in our lives—this is one of our greatest purposes—and to spread joy to our fellow humans in this world, and even to animals. I am a big animal lover. My dog brings such joy to me, and I know I give him joy. Joy is something that is worth practicing.

Peace; there's no law against it. Peace is something that this world is longing for. When everyone is asked "If you could have one thing?" world peace is one of the top things that come to mind. Why do we want that? Because it's an ideal way to live.

This means practicing peace in your life, in your relationships, even being at peace with your money—again, not feeling envy, not feeling lust, avoiding Mammon; peace overcomes these things.

Forbearance is another key word there is no law against. Forbearance means that even if you are owed something, you don't necessarily have to collect. It's the ability to pass on by and let it go. Many people would call, or complain; they would spend hours and hours of their life complaining. But if you are okay to accept it and move past it, you will have more peace and more joy.

If you have more peace and more joy, you will have more love. See how this works?

Kindness is important. It is easy to say, "I love everybody," but what about when you first meet someone and there is some friction? Maybe they have a bad attitude. It's hard to immediately love them, but, ideally, you can always practice kindness.

There is no law against kindness. There is no law against **goodness.** There is no law against **gentleness.**

Of course, one that is significant to all the above beautiful fruits of the spirit is **self-control**.

If you are in control of your mind, your body and your actions, you can share a lot more love, joy, peace, forbearance, kindness, goodness and gentleness.

The last one is **patience.** Patience is good to have in your life. If you are patient with others, they will most likely be patient with you. Do not ask the universe for patience or you may be taught a lesson. I asked for that only once, and I spent years being strengthened through testing! The way to learn patience is through long suffering. I have never asked for that one again.

Not everything is going to come right away, even when the advanced law of attraction is working in your life. Some things are just not meant to be at this time, or maybe you are not ready for them. In my seminars, I actually teach you how to become ready faster. If you want to get there faster, then I suggest you check out www.thespeakerscompany.com

Is It Easy?

Everyone is different. For some, getting rid of things on the bad side won't be too hard. They will recognize a few and start to work on them. For others, it may feel like the hardest thing they will ever do. If that is you, then you need to know that it is rooted deep in your life and will take some time to eliminate, but you can do it, and it is better to start now.

You have taken the most important first step: you have become aware of it. Without knowing what to change, how do you even begin? The next step is choice. Choose to let go of the bad and start to walk in the good.

The third step is the hardest: catching yourself doing it and forcing yourself to walk in a different spirit. The more you do it, the easier it becomes. Practice makes perfect.

In the next chapter we will take what you have learned here and teach you how to use the advanced law of attraction to change your life. You always have to learn the basics before you can move on to more advanced learning. You will be amazed at what happens next!

Jeff Ramsperger

CHAPTER 5:

THE ADVANCED LAW OF ATTRACTION, PART 2 – THE GOD MODULE

A person is only limited by the thoughts that he chooses.

James Allen

Many people find the concept of the advanced law of attraction difficult to wrap their heads around at first. It is counter-intuitive to what the world teaches us. That is why so few people attain it. I hope that the last chapter opened your eyes and let you see there is a different way to live your life.

Now are you ready for the abundance to come? Great! Let's get started.

Once you understand the basics and have begun to implement them into your life, you can move on to the topic of this chapter: The God module.

You are so powerful. You are more powerful than an atomic bomb.

A hydrogen bomb is one thousand times more powerful than the atomic bomb that was dropped on Hiroshima, and everyone in the world saw how powerful that is. It is almost unimaginable power.

How does it work? Let me explain. Your body is 70 percent water: $H2O$—hydrogen is the H in $H2O$. There is enough hydrogen in you, if it were harnessed, to power a country for an entire day.

Yes, when I say power a country, I mean every city, every street light. If there is an electric train, that's included. You have that much power inside of you. You were designed with so much power. Imagine the power of your mind if it could be fully realized and harnessed!

The God module is essentially what makes the advanced law of attraction work. It is common knowledge that although we are capable of using our whole brain, we use only about ten percent of its capacity. Can you imagine the possibilities if we could use its full capacity? Unfortunately, if you are waiting for the answer on how to do that, it's not going to come in this book, although if you are looking for an entertaining movie that shows what can happen, watch *Lucy*, starring Scarlett Johansson.

Half of that 10 percent is used for logic, creation and emotions; this is the active part of your brain. The other 5 percent is scientifically dubbed "the God module." The God module is an antenna in your brain that is constantly seeking out your origins and communicating. Every single thought is communicated.

One way to explain this is that God/the universe has a customer service department. When you ask the universe for something, the customer service department is always listening and ready to deliver.

For instance, if you have a negative emotion connected to driving and say, "I hate traffic," the customer service department says, "Okay, deliver more traffic." Or if you say, "Man, I love my mom's lasagna," all of a sudden, your mom calls and says, "I made you lasagna."

This is how God/the universe customer service department works. Your thoughts go out there, and they don't have to be spoken out loud. Your thoughts actually go out and the universe or customer service is ready to send more of whatever you are asking for.

So, if you are a negative person, it sends more negativity. If you are a positive person, it sends more positivity. If you are a super-positive person, a really negative person really won't be around you long. Adversely, if you are a really negative person, the positive person is going to be repelled from you.

We must guard our thoughts. That's why I spent so much time working on some of the negative things — the fears and emotions that control our thoughts — and why I talked about the five scripts. Your emotions and your emotional state control your thoughts. It's all of these things combined that help you be in more control of your mind.

Your thoughts travel and have influence around the world, even on the moon. Think of it this way. Your thoughts are frequencies that go out. It has been proven that radio and TV frequencies travel out into space, so why can't your thoughts travel around the world?

It has been tested, and it has been proven that your thoughts can control actions and reactions from around the world if they are on the right frequency.

When I gave the example at the beginning of the last chapter about thinking about a long-lost friend ... well, that long-lost friend could be in Singapore, but they just happen to think of you or call you or reach out to you exactly when you thought of it or soon after. That person was able to receive the frequency of your thought.

THE GOD MODULE AND FAITH

When we communicate with this customer service department of the universe, with God, our faith is one of the biggest limiting factors.

We've all heard of that incident when a child is trapped underneath a car, or something like that, and a frail mother lifts up one side of the car and the child escapes.

If the mother had time to sit and think about it, there's no way she could have lifted the car. But because she didn't have time, and she just believed she had to get her child out from underneath the car, she was able to do it. There was no other choice; otherwise her child could have died.

The more you practice this and stretch your limits and control your mind and believe and have faith, the stronger you will get, and the more evidence you will see, which will give you more confidence and you will get to the next level again. Higher and higher. More stuff will start appearing.

When that happens, be thankful. Recognize it. Say thank you. Who wants to keep giving you gifts if you are not appreciative? This is how the God module works.

In the spiritual universe, if you speak out loud, everybody can hear—evil spirits, good spirits, and of course anyone in the surrounding area. And word can travel, because they can all hear it and they can tell someone else.

Your thoughts cannot be heard by Mammon, because he cannot understand the frequency of thought. The evil inside him limits his abilities. Only God can read and know your thoughts, because He knows everything. Your spoken words have power; that is why it is better to never speak the negative thoughts in your head.

MORE ON THE GOD MODULE

I hope you are realizing by this point that everything is interconnected. The more you can integrate these different themes, which I am sharing in this book, the more effective you will be.

In working with your God module and assuming you want to attract affluence, you want to attract good health, you want to attract better people in your life, you want to attract more holidays into your life, you want to attract all of these beautiful things you were meant to have that bring you joy, peace and the positive fruits of the spirit, you must be at cause and not at effect and must work in the spirit.

Now, working in the spirit takes almost no energy. It's just having control over your life and knowing what is in your mind. It's limiting the garbage that goes in and bringing in more of the positive. Then it's being at cause and asking for these things to be revealed in your life. Be creative, because you are a creator. You can create your own reality; oftentimes it will be manifest.

The spiritual controls the physical. If there is no life force in this world, there's nothing happening. The spiritual is in complete control.

However, when you create something in your mind, when you visualize it, when you put it out there to the customer service department, you must act. You need to start walking toward it and believing it will come at some point in your life. If it doesn't happen instantly, don't say, "Well, that didn't work." The universe will say, "Okay, send this person more of what didn't work."

You have to believe.

Do not let limiting beliefs stop you. Just bring the creative into your life and know it will happen. When, you ask? Well, that depends. It will happen when the time is right. You might think the time is right, but God might know something a little bit better.

When attracting affluence and other positive things into your life, do not wish. "Oh, I wish I had that." Wishing is weak. Wishing is bringing in a limiting belief that has zero faith. The universe says, "Okay, he wants to wish. Give him more wishes." It doesn't mean it becomes real—do not wish.

THE GREAT BARRIER

When you have learned to take action and not react and at cause rather than at effect, things will start to go the right way, you are about to make the biggest breakthrough of your life.

Here comes the great barrier. I call it the great barrier because whenever you are about to go to the next level, you are going to be challenged. Are you really ready to go to the next level? Can you handle going to the next level? Is it good for you, or would having a lot of money ruin you? There is a protective barrier that God, or the universe, if that is your belief, puts up.

This great barrier is where most people turn back. You're getting there, things are going in the right direction, and all of a sudden there is a huge problem. Many people (but not you) will listen to that voice in their head, which comes from fears and weaknesses, and say it is too difficult.

They say to the universe, "I can't get past it," and the universe says, "Okay, send more belief that they can't get past."

Or they can't solve the problem. Or other negative influencers around them say, "You can't do that, you come from poverty," or "You can't do that, you don't have the education," or "You can't do that, you don't have enough money," and they believe them.

This could be the barrier. The barrier appears in many different forms. I would venture to say that 90 percent of the population turns back. They let fears and emotions get in the way. But you now have the knowledge. You can *break out* and *through* this barrier.

When you break through that barrier to reach the next level, you are given more tools in your toolkit, and more things start to happen.

ATTRACTING AND PERSUADING

When I talk about being at cause and not being at effect, notice how I am repeating these words? I am doing that, so it really sinks deep into your being.

I now want to put the idea into some new words: "attracting" and "persuading." Other words for attracting and persuading are "sales" and "marketing." I am speaking about the advanced law of attraction. Attraction is attracting these things into your life.

Attracting could be marketing. You need to put in some physical effort if you really want to manifest things that are huge in your life. You want those dreams to become reality, and it's nice to think it and it's nice to say thank you when you start to see things coming, but you must work toward it. So, if you want to attract, it's one thing to say to the universe, "Send me more clients," and it's another to walk toward it— that could be marketing.

When you market to get new clients they have to be persuaded. How do you persuade them? Well, you have to get their confidence. Remember, if you want someone to give you money, you need agreement and confidence. That is sales and marketing. Sales and marketing are the physical aspects of working with the advanced law of attraction.

Everything in life is sales. If you are trying to attract a new mate into your life, if you are courting someone, you are in sales. You have to be at the top of your game as everything in life is sales. You say you hate sales? The universe will send more hated sales to you.

Are you getting the point?

You must start to love sales and it might not be what the world has painted a picture of. Everyone hates that sleezy salesperson who tries to sell you something you don't want. That's not ethical sales. You want to attract ethical money.

Ethical money is the right thing to attract. Everything is sales. "But I am a machine-shop operator. How I am doing sales?" Well, you went to the interview, didn't you? Every day, when you see your boss, you want to make a good impression. If they think you are a bum, you are not going to last long. You're in sales constantly, whether you realize it or not.

Now, if we can agree that you are in sales, and you need to embody the physical attributes that go along with the spiritual attributes of attracting things into your life and working with agreement and confidence as sales and marketing, then you need to sell.

Here are some golden rules for sales:

Rule #1: Only sell what you truly believe in. If you do not fully believe in a product, you will not be successful selling it. If you are trying to court someone and you don't really believe in yourself, you are not going to get the person you want; they are not going to believe in you either.

If you are going to a job interview and you really don't believe you can perform the tasks of that job, they will not hire you. Only sell what you truly believe in.

Rule#2: Sales is helping people. It's not a bad thing when it's performed properly. In this day and age, when there is a ton of information available at your fingertips, reviews on products, and so much information, people need help making the right decision.

Now, because you are selling only what you truly believe in, and because you truly believe in it, you are the expert in it; all you have to do is help someone make the right decision. Perhaps the right decision for them is not to use your product.

In fact, there is a saying in business: sometimes the best client is the one you fire. But if it is the right product for them, just help them make the decision.

By the way, don't sell from your own pocket. Just because you can't afford it, it doesn't mean someone else can't; don't judge them. In fact, one of my biggest clients was a guy who looked like he had nothing. Turned out he was a multi-multi-millionaire. Never judge.

Rule #3: Ask for the money. It saddens me when I see a salesperson say, "When you make up your mind, here's my card." That's okay if someone isn't sure and you haven't been able to help them reach that decision—it's fine if they walk away. Perhaps they do really need to discuss it with their spouse or check with their bank manager to see if they have enough money. There are all kinds of reasons why someone might not buy on the spot, but it's your job to ask for the money.

How do you ask for the money? Ask them if this is the right product for them. In fact, ask lots of questions. The client should do most of the talking. The best salespeople just ask the questions and the client will tell them what they want or need. If the client is unsure, by asking questions and using your expertise you will be able to guide them to the best decision.

Now that you have all kinds of learning in the spirit and you have the physical tools, you are ready to go out and make a lot more. But there is one last obstacle.

Your heart and mind must agree. Emotions are in your heart, and your heart and mind are connected. I want to ask you a question. Would you sleep with someone who kept telling you, "You can't do this?" Would you sleep with someone who says, "You are not good enough?" Would you sleep with someone who constantly reminds you that you are not educated enough or that you don't have enough money?

You do sleep with yourself, right?

TYING IT ALL TOGETHER

The advanced law of attraction is not just one thing. It is a lifestyle where the spiritual, the physical, your mind and your heart, are all in alignment. When that happens, abundance begins. Don't get discouraged if you are not there yet.

Everyone is on a journey, and the most essential thing is that you continue to move forward. Some days it may feel like you are moving backward, and you probably are, but remember an arrow is only propelled forward at great speed after being pulled back at great pressure. If that is you, take courage. Your time is quickly coming.

In Section 2 of this book, we are going to look at the actions you can take to create success and abundance in your life. I will get down to the nitty-gritty of what it takes to create financial freedom in your life

Jeff Ramsperger

SECTION 2:

THE ROAD TO WEALTH, BUSINESS

Jeff Ramsperger

CHAPTER 6:

DELEGATION AND COMMUNICATION

If you want to do a few small things right, do them yourself. If you want to do great things and make a big impact, learn to delegate.
                                        John C. Maxwell

So far in this book, you've learned that you need to be ready to be wealthy. You've learned that you need to know what your *why* is: your reason to succeed and the compelling factor that will keep you motivated.

You've also learned what money is and the differences between money, riches, and wealth. I've taught you about being a good steward and how important that is. You've learned about spiritual and physical agreement. I covered cause and effect and how you always want to be at cause. You've learned that relationships are your true net worth and about the ethics of wealth.

Then we got into some amazing stuff about your mind actually attracting and creating your own economy; you could bring something wonderful to your life by just thinking it. There is little effort in the spiritual realm and there's more effort in the physical realm...

Now we are going to bridge the gap between the spiritual and the physical. I could give you all the spiritual knowledge in the world, but if you don't have physicalaction items you will not have a complete system. This book is intended to be a system and to systematically give you a path to follow from having money to having riches, to wealth, and eventually your perfect life.

In this chapter, we're going to cover what it takes to get your actions operating more efficiently as well as how you can communicate to help others on your team, get your life running efficiently, ready to do business and generate wealth.

CLEAN UP YOUR MESSES AND CLOSE OPEN CYCLES

In Chapter 2, I talked about procrastination being a gift to you. It teaches you what you should be doing and what you should not be doing. It helps you realize what your strengths and weaknesses are.

In this chapter I want to go a couple steps further and cover something my mentor taught me that absolutely changed my life. When he first said it to me, it affected me so deeply that it changed my outlook on life, and my habits.

It's called cleaning up your messes and closing open cycles.

What this means is that everyone has messes in their life. Messes might not be exactly what you perceive. Certainly, untidiness is a mess, but unresolved situations in your life are messes, too. You may have thought, "Oh, I have to call that person," but you've been putting it off.

Or, "I promised this person I would drop something off," and you've been putting that off. Or, "We've wanted to get together for the longest time, but we just haven't made that connection." You've got all of these things running as open cycles in your mind, and they slow you down.

Take, for example, your computer. When it's running you will see all of your open items at the bottom of the screen. If you have a thousand items open at once, how fast is your computer going to be running? How effectively is the processing power of that computer?

Your mind operates the same way.

I am going to use a personal example: my office was messy. The strain that that put on my life was incredible. I didn't realize it until my mentor taught me this. Because it was always in the back of my mind, "I have to clean my office," it was an open cycle. It was an open file operating in my mind, constantly using my mind's resources.

I would be willing to say that you have over a thousand open cycles. Some of them are not at the top of your mind; some have been put off for so long you can't even recall them. You've probably got ten or fifteen immediate open cycles, maybe even more, maybe twenty-five to fifty open cycles, that are just slowing down your processing power.

It slows your ability to make informed decisions. It slows your ability to learn. It certainly slows down the way you attract good things to your life. It dampens down that God module. It slows down everything in your life.

You need to start closing those files, and delegating is one of the best ways to do that. If you've been procrastinating and putting off things for a long time, get someone else to do it, or just write them down as they come to mind and get rid of them.

It's so much faster to make that phone call you promised. It's so much faster to organize that event you have been putting off. It's so much faster to clean up the garage or have someone else clean up your garage for you, than it is to have open cycles slowing down everything in your life.

When you delegate, you're going to find someone who is good at doing the particular task, someone who enjoys doing it. And, by the way, delegation doesn't have to cost you money. The person you are delegating the cleaning of your garage to, or whatever task you have put off, most likely has messes in their life. It's likely that you can fill a void for them and operate in fair exchange. Except you might go further and operate in abundance, which I will talk about in the next chapter.

When you are delegating, communication is everything. There is a mess or an open file in your life that you are not good at dealing with, but you say to yourself, "Well, only an expert can do this, that's why I'm stuck with it, but I don't like doing it; that's why I've put it off for so long." Here is the fix: build a system. Write down a process you only have to do once.

If you are not good at communicating or building processes, go to someone who is good at putting processes together and designing systems. That way, you can delegate at any time those particular tasks, and all someone has to do is read the instructions or follow the system and they will accomplish the task for you. If they move on, you can hand it to the next person.

Now, isn't this wonderful? You can clean up your life and you can start to live life the way you were meant to. You can start attracting more wealth into your life. You're only going to do the things that make you money. Because if you make $40 an hour but you can hire someone to cut your lawn for $10 or $15 an hour, why would you cut your lawn?

Why would you do that? Wouldn't you rather spend your time making that $40 an hour or $100 an hour or $1,000? Why would you be bogged down with tasks like this?

Jivanne and I used to clean our house every Saturday morning. Of course, we would tidy up during the week, but we would do a thorough cleaning every Saturday morning. It would take us four or five hours of our precious time. Now, we have someone at a very reasonable price who does a much better job than we ever did, and it takes the same amount of time for one person to clean our house as it did for the two of us. So, delegate, delegate, delegate.

If you are delegating in your business or creating a power team of people who are not employees (whom I would call subcontractors or people who work to help grow your business), you need to pay very close attention to some key points.

The first is that you want to hold the paper. What I mean by that is all things should surround you. You should place yourself as the person in charge. The people you delegate to, although they might be working toward the same cooperative goal—which is your goal, because you have assembled the team— don't necessarily know each other, but they are working for you. You need to hold the paper. That means you hold the policy, you hold the strategic plan to communicate their roles with expertise. Be strategic in your planning of this.

Strategic planning is the process of defining your strategy, or direction and making decisions on the allocation of resources to this plan. This is the plan your team will operate under.

Your employees or the team of people you delegate to will follow your communication and follow your policies to exact standards. You need to set your expectations and communicate with them very clearly. If someone does not agree with your expectations, they are not the right person to fulfil them. Communication is everything in delegation.

The last point I would like to make about delegation relates to pay. Pay your employees or your team very well. Loyalty can't be bought, but if you want to create a long-lasting team of excellence, then pay them the most that you can. As your business grows, reward them for their hard work. Let them see that as the business prospers so do they. It gives them motivation to do more for you.

Now that we have got your mind functioning properly, you've learned how to attract and use it to create wealth and bring good things to you, you've learned about the God module, you've learned how to communicate and delegate some of the tasks and open files that have bogged down your life and stopped your productivity. In the next chapter I am going to get into business fundamentals.

These fundamentals are an understanding of business common sense. It can apply to any business. Whether you have an existing business, you are starting a business, or you are an employee, you are going to get great benefit from the next chapter.

Jeff Ramsperger

CHAPTER 7:

BUSINESS FUNDAMENTALS

*"Step out of the history that is holding you back.
Step into the new story you are willing to create."*
Oprah Winfrey

Business is a way to generate wealth. It is how you put action to what you have learned in Section 1 of this book. Business can be perceived in many ways, but the way I like to look at it is as a system of reoccurring and predictable revenue that grows every year. A few years ago, I read the book Rich Dad, Poor Dad by Robert Kiyosaki, and then I read the next one, called The Cashflow Quadrant. Those two books had a profound effect on my life and how I was to become wealthy. After reading the second one I went out and started in real estate.

One of the big themes in these books is the cash-flow quadrant. Robert shows it as a graph containing the letters E, S, B and I. It is essential to understand how the clash-flow quadrant works and which side of the cash-flow quadrant makes money and which side doesn't. Let's look at each one.

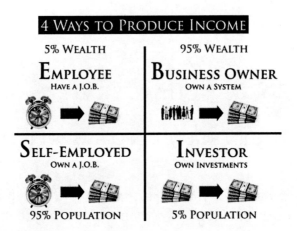

E stands for employee. This is someone who goes to work every day and gets a regular paycheque. The job could be low-paying or it could be high-paying, but it is a job, and it is unlikely that having a job alone will help you achieve riches or wealth.

My opinion is that it is great to be an employee, particularly if you love your job and you make decent money at it. It's what you do with your money at the end of the day that counts and employing investment strategies using or leveraging your steady paycheque can be an excellent choice to move toward riches or wealth.

The letter S, also on the left side of the cash-flow quadrant, stands for self-employed. Many people will describe being self-employed as buying yourself a job, and it comes with some very good pros, like possible tax savings and flexible hours. But it also has some cons. Many self-employed people end up working longer hours, assume greater risks, have to deal with the paperwork, and it is much harder to borrow money as a self-employed person.

Having said that, a small business can often grow into a large business if you use proper business practices. Unfortunately, most self-employed people do not learn proper management structures and how to measure by statistics, and they often don't run the business by the numbers. To be in business, numbers are everything if you ever want to grow, and certainly if you want to succeed.

On the right side of the cash-flow quadrant you see the letter B, which stands for business. Robert Kiyosaki describes this as a larger business. I will define it as a business that is able to run without you, the owner, present and is predictably profitable. Having a scalable business with many employees is a wonderful way to generate riches or wealth. If it is your company, you must manage by the numbers, and you should be constantly measuring statistics to ensure sustainable growth.

The letter I is also on the right side of the cash-flow quadrant and it stands for investment. This is where your money is working for you and generating passive income. Think of a business that can run itself without you being there and still generate money. Investing is the same thing. It allows you to receive money based on your educated investments. Most people who have become rich or wealthy have a combination of business and investments.

Now I want you to notice that the left side of the cash-flow quadrant is where your ability to become wealthy is limited. However, on the right side is where most of the money in the world is made. As you plot out your future, it is worthwhile to look at the quadrant and decide where you really want to be. As you plot out your future, it is worthwhile to look at this and decide where you really want to be. Immediately you might think, *I am just an employee, or self-employed, and I cannot get to the right side of the cash-flow quadrant.* If you think that way, you are wrong, and you are telling the universe to send more, "I can't do it," your way. The rest of this book will show you how to make the transition.

NO MONEY

In business everyone has heard the saying, "It takes money to make money." Money speeds up the process, but you can make money starting with nothing. This is the street-smarts aspect of business.

The traditional way of starting a business is to decide what your product is, develop your product, come up with a basic business structure, have your product ready to go, and then start selling it. No wonder most new businesses go out of business. Think about the traditional method for a moment, and how much money, time and effort is put into thinking of a product, then creating the product, then stocking the product, and then waiting for sales.

There is something called a burn rate. This is simply the rate at which you burn through cash. If you come up with an idea, invest money into it and have your whole business set up before you make any sales, you could be burning through cash for months or even years.

The street-smart person comes up with a great idea and then goes to sell it. Have you ever seen one of those infomercials where they have this great product and it's at a great price and very tempting, and they get lots of orders, but the fine print onscreen says to allow six to eight weeks for delivery? This is how smart business people operate. They only pay for a demo model and the commercials and don't manufacture the product until they have enough sales to pay for the rest.

A purchase order or actual orders from clients with their credit card information is something you can take to the bank or any other type of lender and get money to fulfill the order as long as the numbers make sense.

Remember the example I gave in the earlier chapter about my daughter starting a website-building business. She had basic knowledge, figured out the pricing and went out and sold it. She got deposits and then invested in the tools to deliver the product. She removed much of the risk from starting a new small business.

Other examples of making money without having money to start are found in business or real estate. If you can find a deal and make money in the buy, you can find someone to invest in it for a share of the profits. If someone came to me and said they found a house that is worth $350,000 and they can get it for $280,000, after performing my due diligence I would pay them a generous finder's fee. So, it is possible to make money without having money, but it does take effort.

GOAL SETTING

Setting goals is something that must be done. I was told so many times the importance of setting goals, and I would vaguely think of some goals and then not do anything with them. Guess what happened? That's right, nothing. I never achieved any of them.

"You don't need to be a genius or a visionary, or even a college graduate for that matter, to be successful. You just need a framework and a dream."

Michael Dell

If you do not know your destination, how do you plan to get there? Here is a simple way to look at goals so they are not overwhelming. What is your endgame? How much is enough to live out your perfect life? It would be easy to say, "I need a billion dollars," and for some of you that might be possible, but I would prefer to stay with some realistic but highly aggressive goals.

For example, I learned that being rich means having an annual income in the United States of about $250,000 or $350,000 in Canada. This is a goal that can be achieved by taking action with a lot of positivity and some time. You need to set out what your goal will be. One of the best ways to achieve your goals is to take that end result and start working backward.

As an investor with a goal of $100,000 passive income, how many doors would I need to own to have that money come in? Depending on the real estate strategy you use, it could be twenty-five doors, or it could be a hundred doors, but I will tell you this is totally achievable not only in real estate but in other types of investments and in business as well. Later on, in this book, I will discuss investment strategies with you in detail and help you choose the one that is right for you. Of course, I will let you know the spiritual viewpoint on each of these as well.

USP

One of the first things to ask when starting a business or increasing your existing business is, what is your unique selling proposition (USP)?

What is unique about you as the face of the company or as the brand of the company? What separates you from others in your industry? For instance, if you are a home builder, what type are you? There are tract home builders, there are commercial home builders and there are luxury home builders.

If you are, for instance, a luxury home builder, what separates you from the other luxury home builders in the industry? Every luxury home builder uses the same finishes, the same quality materials. Everyone uses granite countertops. Everyone uses better appliances and better finishes throughout the home.

But if you were the custom home builder that put in quiet plumbing, and it could be a guarantee that if you are in an adjoining room you will never hear a flush or hear the water moving through the pipes, that would be a unique selling proposition that separates you from everybody else in the field.

Another example would be if you're a car salesman. Perhaps you're a car salesperson who has a book, and your book could be *How to Get Maximum Performance*

Out of Your Vehicle and Better Financing. Or *How to Select the Right Car for You.* Or perhaps it's about customer service, even if it's just a mini book. You can distinguish yourself as that person.

I would be remiss if I did not include employees in this. As an employee, what is your unique selling proposition? As an employee, how do you stand out? If you do not stand out of the crowd, you will not get that promotion, you will not get that pay raise. So, you, as an employee, need to improve your brand and be noticed.

One of the traps that employees can fall into is staying late every night. Well, that could be noticed as a good thing, but if you stay late every night, maybe it's just expected; maybe the owner thinks you are just a slow worker.

Instead, how about always completing projects on time and delivering them with a smile and making sure that that is noticed? I'm delivering on time, and by the way I exceeded your expectations. These are all great things that can help you determine what your unique selling proposition is.

AN EXCHANGE IN ABUNDANCE

In business and in life there are levels of exchange. What is an exchange?

Everything in business is an exchange. An exchange is trading a product for something of equivalent value or trading a service for something of equivalent value. In other words, if you are a plumber, you are exchanging plumbing services and hardware for a fair amount of money.

When you are developing your products in your business or place of employment (even as an employee you have products), you need to come up with your most valuable product first. This doesn't mean you go out and create it, spend the money, load up your garage and then try to sell it, as previously mentioned. But you need to evaluate what your most valuable product is. It's also good to have secondary products for those who cannot afford your top product.

There are four levels of exchange.

This is a great lesson I learned from one of my mentors. Examine these four levels and see how the teaching can be applied in your life or business. If you operate in the highest one, money and good things will come your way continuously.

The lowest level of exchange is called criminal or rip-off. Criminal or rip-off exchange is when you give something of value and get nothing in return. Or vice versa. (We are not talking about charity; charity is separate, and I believe in charity.)

Criminal exchange is when you support someone or give someone—for instance, a homeless person on the street (this could sound controversial)—money and get nothing in return. You are helping that person do nothing with their life. You are helping this person stay the way they are or get worse, so it has an unintended effect.

I understand that the homeless person may be mentally ill or have other challenges, but there are programs, charities, that know how to properly disperse assistance, how to properly help these people.

Some of the people you see at the side of highways, I've been told, make up to $40 an hour in cash. You are helping that person never get a job, and they are not contributing to society. They are not paying tax on that. (I'm assuming they are not paying tax on it.) Criminal exchange is not a good exchange and is something that should be avoided.

You don't want to receive criminal exchange, because then the person giving you something for nothing is making a criminal of you. This does not mean that you cannot accept a gift. A gift is not criminal exchange.

The second level of exchange is partial. Partial exchange is when you pay for something but do not receive full value with what you get. Have you ever been to a fast-food restaurant and looked at the menus above the counter where you order? You see a big, thick, juicy burger, but when you get your burger it is about half the size of the one in the picture. You were deceived.

Now, you are still accepting the partial exchange. If it's a place you frequent, you accept partial exchange, and perhaps it moves into the next level, at least in your mind or your acceptance.

Or have you ever ordered something on the Internet, or off the TV from one of these infomercials, and it really didn't live up to what was promised? They did give you what they said they would, but it wasn't as good.

For instance, you order a cleaning product and it says it will clean everything effortlessly. It's a good cleaning product, but it certainly isn't effortless—I still have to scrub my bathtub with it. That is partial exchange.

There are many, many companies operating in partial exchange, and when you are operating in partial exchange it is counter-survival. This means the company will last for a while, but it is going downhill. Unless it reinvents itself, most likely it will go out of business.

So, in business or even as an employee, partial exchange is not where you want to be.

The next level is called fair exchange. This is where I would say the majority of successful companies are. In fair exchange, just as the title implies, you exchange money and you get exactly what you paid for. It meets your expectations. It delivers on its promises. Nothing more, nothing less. Fair exchange.

The last level of exchange is the most important.

The last one is called exchange in abundance. When you exchange in abundance, your business will skyrocket. Your brand will skyrocket. You will have trouble stopping the money from coming in. You will have referrals.

People will brag about your product or service without you asking them to. People will say, "You need to work with this person or company; I couldn't believe how great they were." They will go out of their way to promote you. Here is how it works:

If I were selling sunglasses, and they were everything you expected, that is fair exchange. However, if I included a $20 cleaning kit and you did not expect it, that is abundance.

An exchange in abundance is something that was not expected. It's a surprise; it creates a WOW feeling when someone receives the product. This is delivering in exchange of abundance.

In writing this book, I am operating in the exchange of abundance. I am exchanging an incredible amount of information for a very reasonable price. I am also including bonuses that you can get on my website. www.affinitytoaffluence.com

Now, it was not mentioned on the cover that you will get these. A lot of authors do that. I am not doing that, because I want to operate in exchange of abundance.

PAY ON PERFORMANCE

Another key in starting a business or ramping up your existing business is paying on performance.

Many businesses run on an hourly pay or salary system. However, I would quickly move them to pay on performance.

Pay on performance gives an opportunity for someone to operate in exchange of abundance. It gives them an opportunity to be rewarded for going the extra mile. If they perform better, you are making more money.

The following example shows how to introduce pay on performance. Employee X makes $60,000 a year. With pay on performance, continuing to do exactly what they are doing, they will still make $60,000 a year. However, if they increase sales or productivity, whatever the job, and it creates additional revenue, then they will get a share in that revenue.

So, instead of paying $60,000, you might be dangling a carrot for another $20,000 a year. That is a significant amount of money for a family or for a single person.

I encourage you to give those incentives to people. Allow them to shine, allow them to use their special gifts, and this will help your business ramp up, and ramp up fast.

THE BUSINESS-CONSULTANT FIX

If you run a business that's getting by, you are just doing the day-to-day, and not much changes, I will refer you to the earlier chapter that talks about the complacency trap.

In this complacency trap you are actually in counter-survival. You're limiting the duration of your business, because the world is constantly changing — you must be able to create change constantly.

Many businesses either go for additional financing or bring in a business consultant, someone who can look from outside the walls and make some changes to help the business grow and increase profits.

In fact, if you watch popular TV shows like *Dragons' Den* in Canada or *Shark Tank* in the United States, you see these very savvy business people come into a business, make a slight adjustment and all of a sudden the business is booming.

Well, good news. I am going to tell you the number-one fix in business that will completely change your income levels and help you grow. Every business has three sections to it. Even if it's a service-based business.

The Three Elements of Business

1. Manufacturing: 10% of Company Resources

Now, even if you are service-based and don't manufacture a product, you always have manufacturing in your business.

You have to manufacture documents; you have to manufacture policies, business systems, paper flow. All of these different things are in your business, and a constant part of your business is manufacturing these things.

2. Operations: 65% of Company Resources

Operations are the backbone — your administration, things that happen in the business. Your billing cycle and management cycle are examples of your operations.

Most companies spend about 10 percent of resources, meaning they use people or staff or time, in operations.

3. Sales: 25% of Company Resources

Sales is seemingly the most important part of your business because without sales you wouldn't have a business. It's better to prioritize sales, because if you have lots of sales, you can solve the manufacturing and operations part of your business.

You can solve all problems by having income. If you have lots of income, you can hire the right people to take care of the manufacturing and operations part of your business.

Most businesses operate this way; 10 percent of their business resources is allocated to manufacturing, 65 percent is allocated to operations and 25 percent of your time or resources is dedicated to sales.

Here is the fix:

You need to reverse the numbers for sales and operations. Most businesses are operating the opposite way: the amount of assets, time and resources allocated to operations and sales is backwards.

I know it's shocking. Most businesses are operating the opposite way: they have operations and sales percentage of assets, times and resources backward. Just change that, and it will revolutionize your new business.

If it's an existing business, change that. Look at your business right now. These numbers are accurate for most businesses out there. Flip the numbers for operations and sales and watch your business skyrocket.

Resource Allocation	Percentage of Time (most businesses	The FIX Percentage of Time
Manufacturing	10%	10%
Operations	65%	25%
Sales	25%	65%

You Must Have an Internet Strategy

To conclude this chapter, I want to address the type of business and the changing times we are in. The market is changing dramatically. Retail is not as relevant as it once was. Many services are not as relevant as they once were. The Internet has changed the world.

As part of your business, no matter what type of business it is, you really should have the Internet. Perhaps the Internet could sell a product or service and create passive income for your business 24/7, because the Internet is always operating. Or perhaps the internet is simply generating leads for your business.

It is crucial in today's economy to have the Internet as part of your business. When I say that, I don't mean putting up a website that no one will ever see. If no one can find your website, your website does not exist.

If you think just handing out a business card and getting people to your website is enough, you are wrong. Your website needs to be generating leads or generating income or both.

Please take the time to talk to an expert. Bring in that team member who is crucial to your business and pay them fairly or even abundantly to get their best effort. It will be money well spent, and it will help you achieve your goals.

Hold the Paper

Who makes the most money in any given business? The answer in most cases is the person who holds the paper. Let me explain. At the top of an organization is the person who takes ultimate responsibility for the success or failure of the business. This is the person who usually makes the most money—obvious, right?

There are exceptions. Perhaps the top salesperson who keeps bringing the large deals makes more. Holding the big deals or profits is also holding the paper. As a CEO, if I have a salesperson who makes more than I do because they are bringing so much profitability to the company, I would encourage that person to keep going. No pride is at stake; I do not have to be the highest paid.

Here is the key. If you want to be super successful in business, hold the paper! This comes with responsibility, whether you are the CEO or the top salesperson. It is possible to "get lucky" in business, have the right product or service at the right time, but to sustain continued growth and longevity you need to take the responsibility of holding the paper.

This means, start to love organizational charts, systems, policies and statistics. Manage your business this way, constantly monitoring and comparing. When a deficiency is identified, assign a policy fix to it and continue to monitor. This sounds very complicated, but the opposite is true. When these are in place, life gets much easier, and the success rate for your business will multiply.

In the next chapter I'm going to give you some insight on one of the most important skills you can learn. I am going to make it an easy read. I've read several weighty books on the subject, and I am going to give you what my life experience has taught me are the top points that will help you move your business forward and help your life in general.. It's a short chapter, so don't delay. It ties in really well with what you have just read. Just get this one done and then take a break.

CHAPTER 8:

NETWORKING AND NEGOTIATION

Let us never negotiate out of fear. But let us never fear to negotiate.

John F. Kennedy

Gary had a decision to make, and it would change his life. He had two choices: figure out how to make his business work or close the doors and try to get a job.

When he first started his business, he felt invincible. This was his dream, and he was willing to invest in it. He took money out of his savings to get everything he needed to get going. His website and business cards were exquisite, he had a business plan that would put most business owners to shame, he had set up a home office that was professional and artistic at the same time and he had bought a package deal where he got a virtual assistant for a year. He was set.

That is when things turned south. He couldn't seem to get the high-paying customers he needed to make his business a success. He went to every networking meeting he could. He handed out what seemed like thousands of business cards. He paid for local advertising. Nothing he did worked. He got a few clients for his low-end service, but that wasn't enough to even pay back his savings, let alone make a profit.

He couldn't understand what was wrong. His friend Rob, who lived a few hours away, had started a business selling the same type of service as Gary around the same time and was doing great. His business was thriving and making a profit. Gary didn't know what he was doing wrong, but he was going to find out. It was either that or shut the business for good.

He picked up the phone and dialed his friend...

THE FIRST VITAL BUSINESS SKILL

Why was Gary's business failing while Rob's succeeded? The answer is simple. Rob had two skills that Gary didn't even know about, let alone master. If you are a solopreneur, freelancer, in the real estate or financial industry, or a small-business owner, these two skills are essential if you want your business to stay alive. You must be able to network, and you must be able to negotiate. Without those skills, you are sunk.

Remember earlier in the book when I talked about your network being your net worth? As your network grows, so does your influence and your credibility, which then allows you to grow your network further. Imagine it as an upward spiral that gets bigger the higher you go.

At each level, your ability to bring in new business grows exponentially. That is why it seems like some businesses take big leaps forward—they are seeing the results of their new, cumulative networking efforts.

Think of it this way. Each person in your network not only represents themselves but all their friends, family, co-workers, clients and/or customers. If you network with people properly, they will not only allow you access to the people you know but will promote you as well. You get enough individuals doing that, and your business will soar.

THE NON-TRADITIONAL
WAY TO NETWORK

Everyone who is new to networking does the same thing. They get the best business cards they can afford, find a local networking meeting, and go there hoping someone will say those magic words: "Can I buy something from you?"

Usually, it goes one of two ways. One, the person is desperate for business and goes to the meeting with dollar signs in their eyes. Everyone can feel it and avoids them. Two, the person is silenced by fear. The person has no idea what they are doing and are afraid of saying the wrong thing, so they do not talk to anyone.

If that is what you have been taught, I suggest you throw that plan in the garbage for good, because it does not work.

I am going to share with you how networking really works. Are you ready? It is never about business, but relationships. I know what you are thinking, "How do I make sales by developing relationships?" The answer is simple. People do business with people they know, like and trust.

Let's say you are looking to have some printing done. You have two printers to choose from. There is one who is slightly closer to you and their prices are lower, but you don't know them and none of your circle has used them.

On the other hand, a good friend of yours owns a printing shop. It is five minutes farther away and the prices are a little bit higher, but you know that your friend will do a great job for you, will probably throw in a freebie, and if there are any problems they will take care of it quickly.

Which one do you choose? Of course, your friend. The same thing applies to your network. As they come to know you and the quality of your service and product, they won't care if someone is closer and cheaper. They will go to you *and* recommend you to others.

Who Do You Network With?

Network with people who can move your business forward. They could be potential clients, or maybe they are above you and know influential people who can make your business rise faster.

How Do You Connect with Those Above You?

You connect by being where they are. Some of the best relationships I've made have been at places you would not have expected.

For instance, on holidays, particularly when you don't cheap out, and you spend the extra thousand dollars to go to a nicer place, you meet a lot of high-quality people. Even on airplanes. Whenever possible I will fly business class, not only for the comforts it affords me but for the quality of person who ends up sitting in that seat next to me.

A lot of these people are prominent business people. Sometimes employees, sometimes running their own businesses, but they are typically higher-level people if their company will pay for them to sit in the business class seat or if they are able to pay for that for themselves. So, putting yourself in the right spot can really help you forge better relationships.

I think back to one time in particular, when I stayed at a very high-end resort. I met people of such high quality that I am confident that the relationships I developed with them will last me the rest of my years.

Some of these people were far above me financially, like multimillionaires. What I found was that as long you are honest and provide value, really rich people will tell you how to get really rich.

It's amazing. They do not keep secrets. Only poor people keep secrets. "Oh, you might find out how I made an extra hundred dollars," says the poor person. "I don't want you to know my side hustle." Rich people aren't like that.

"Listen, here's how I made $20 million last year," one might say. They are glad to share information with you because there are so few people doing what they do; there's no competition when you get to those levels. On this particular vacation I made such incredible contacts.

One person was building a $20-million facility, and in one of my businesses I could really benefit him. He asked me what I did and what my expertise was, and I told him.

"Are you good at it?" he asked. I said, "I'm one of the best at it." Which was a true statement; I really am one of the best in this particular skill set. He said, "You have the job."

Now, he didn't ask what product it was in particular, and he didn't ask how much it cost. When you are dealing with a high-end person like this, here's what they expect: they expect you to have the highest of ethics, they expect that it will be a fair price—it does not have to be the cheapest price, but it has to be at least a fair price—and they expect everything to be problem-free, that you will take care of the details. Which is all part of ethics in business.

Now, I've not performed that job yet. It is coming up and it is in progress, but I can tell you that I plan to operate in abundance. I am building it into this project, so I can give him a WOW at the end, and he will never use anybody else for that task. This one contact will more than cover the cost of my vacations for the next ten years when the project comes to fruition. So, was it worth spending a couple of extra bucks to go to a better place to meet a better quality of people? Absolutely.

Here is the main thing to focus on in networking. Make your goal to develop relationships where you are not afraid to provide value first and get business later. You should never go in with dollar signs in your eyes, because you will never get anywhere.

NEGOTIATION BASICS

Negotiating is one of the skills of utmost importance in your life. No matter whether it is in your daily life or in your business, having a basic understanding of negotiations is critical to your growth and to making money, particularly making money in the buy, which allows you to get off to a good start.

This section on negotiations will be concise, but I will give you the major tenets I have learned. I will also share the titles of two significant books on the topic that changed how I saw negotiations forever. If you need to improve your negotiation skills, then you *need* to study these two books.

The first I will point to is written by George H. Ross, and it's called *Trump-Style Negotiation.*

George Ross is someone I have had the pleasure of meeting and having a couple of conversations with. You might know the name from the TV show *The Apprentice* with Donald Trump. George Ross was always introduced as Trump's right-hand man.

He is a lawyer who had his office right next to Trump's office. Every major deal Trump did, went through Ross, who was not an employee of Trump. He was purposely not an employee so that he could give his true perspective, good or bad, on any given deal.

Ross helped Donald Trump become a multibillionaire. I think he knows a thing or two about negotiations, and certainly Trump has been one of the best negotiators in today's world. Whether you like his style as a president or dislike it, you cannot disregard what he has accomplished in life, and his negotiation skills are incredible.

I will add one other thing about Ross: he is a straight shooter. I had a dream for many years to build my own entertainment venue, and I had it planned out in such a way that I thought it was absolutely brilliant. I was given the opportunity to ask Ross about my idea. I was expecting him to encourage me, "No one has done it like that before. That's going to be great." Instead, he shot down my idea in about thirty seconds and told me I was an idiot if I decided to pursue it.

Now, that upset me, but I shut my mouth and I listened to him. Within forty-eight hours my feelings were less hurt, and I realized he was absolutely right.

Now, I still have this dream, and I plan to fulfil it, but his insight made me look at something I hadn't thought of before, and he was correct. If I had done it the way I originally planned, it would have eventually failed. Because of his wisdom and just a few short sentences, I now have a really great plan that's going to make a ton of money.

Another book I am going to recommend is one I just recently read. It is a brilliant book and will help you greatly in negotiating. It's written by a Canadian man named Stefan Aarnio. He is a real estate mogul, a young man from Winnipeg, and he wrote the book on negotiations called The *Ten Commandments of Negotiation*. In this chapter I am going to share with you its most important tenets to get you started.

The first thing in negotiations is that you must ask. If you do not ask, you will never get, and it's okay to ask in almost any situation. But be prepared for the answer. If you ask and you don't get, then it's up to you. But you do have to ask.

When going into negotiations, you need to prepare. One of the ways to prepare is to simply evaluate the supply and demand for that particular product or service. If the supply is low and the demand is high, you will unlikely be successful in negotiating.

If someone is the very best in the business—let's say they are the best landscaper in the industry and you love the way they do their work, but they're booked up until next year—do you think you will be successful in negotiating a lower price with them?

Probably not.

Here is one of the main tenets of negotiations: if you are not prepared to walk away, your negotiation will probably fail. To be successful in negotiations you must be prepared to walk away.

Now, having said that, even if you are not prepared to walk away, if you have decided you want this product or service you will buy it and the price is fair, it's still okay to ask. If you do not ask, you will never receive.

However, if you ask and they say, "Sorry, the price is the price," then accept the price, because there really is no strength or leverage in negotiations if the supply is small and the demand is high.

One of the other things I find essential in negotiations is to be a nice person. Be someone they want to talk to. Your company is enjoyable. You are not out there to get them, to be a cutthroat. People see that. If you have a good heart in negotiations and you are pleasant, you are more likely to attract more successful negotiations into your life.

Also, many people will disagree with this, but I do not negotiate to kill. I do not negotiate solely to win and get the very best I can out of any given situation. I do not intend to hurt the other person. If I notice that they are maybe a little desperate in business and really need the money, the temptation to take advantage of them is there, but I won't do that.

If they really need the money, leave some skin in the game. If you can make money in the buy, that's a good thing. Leave some fairness in there for the other person. I believe this is an ethical thing, and even though you might have made a bit more money negotiating the kill, I believe that in the long run you will make more money when the other party can say, "That guy was fair. That guy left skin in the game." Don't take advantage of people. Unless they are awful people—then do the best you can.

Negotiating principles

The first is to know the best position possible. Going into a negotiation, you must always have your best-case scenario. If you could get the product or service for "this amount," what would it be?

Also, you need to know the lowest terms you would accept. Know that unless you get this bare-minimum amount or certain things included, you will walk away from the deal.

Knowing your best acceptable position and your least acceptable position is critical in negotiations. You'll know the top spot, you'll know the last spot, and anywhere in between is acceptable to you.

Part of the way to know what your best position and your lowest acceptable position is through research. You must prepare, prepare, prepare for any negotiation. Whether it's a product or service or a real estate deal, you need to prepare. What are your competitors selling for? What have other people paid for this thing in the past? What is the demand for this particular product or service? What is the supply for this product or service?

You need to research these things as well as research the party you are negotiating with. Know who the other party is and what is important to them. Even try to find personal information about them, because you might be able to include things in negotiation that work for them personally and are not directly related to the deal.

Having your preparation and your research done, you can go into the negotiation with confidence.

Having confidence, knowing your best and least positions and knowing your other party and the demand for the product that you are discussing can give you a significant advantage over those you are negotiating with who have not studied this.

Clutter

In negotiation there's a tactic that is very useful. It is called clutter. This is not my term. I believe it came from George Ross and Donald Trump, who used this technique often in their negotiations, and I would suggest it is good for you to use as well.

Let me work with an example: negotiating for a house.

I am going to buy a house. It is an average market, where houses are not selling in two days; they are selling in sixty to ninety days. So, they are selling, but not really fast. When there are no bidding wars or people offering more money for houses, there is usually room for negotiation. Whether it's big or small doesn't matter.

Let's say the house on the market is worth $400,000. Then I might reason, *Well, $400,000 is the most I would pay for this house.* Let's say in the best-case scenario, because the house needs a little bit of work, I might be able to get it for $350,000. But it's in good shape, so I might start there. It's not likely I am going to get the price down to that $350,000.

Now, the house might have a driveway that needs to be redone. Or it might need some minor landscaping to clean things up, or perhaps there's a wall in the house you would want to moved. Maybe a bathroom needs a little freshening up.

These are all things that could be called clutter.

Using this example, you start the negotiation by maybe throwing out $350,000 on this $400,000 listing.

Now, you have to understand, no one else has bid on this house. If someone had, you've lost the negotiation without going to the table.

No one else has bid. You put out a low-ball offer of $350,000. They come back at $390,000. So, they are telling you, "Look, we are willing to negotiate a little bit, but you are way out there with your numbers."

Now, if $390,000 is still within what I am willing to pay, I can start to use clutter. "How about $390,000, but you also refresh that bathroom and redo the driveway?"

They might come back and say, "Okay, I will accept $390,000, but I am not willing to do the driveway. I will refresh the bathroom."

So, you've added a bit more value. Then you can go back to them again and say, "If you are not willing to do the driveway, the walkway from the driveway to the front of the house really could use some refreshing, and I really need this house to be move-in ready, otherwise the house won't work for me. So, how about $390,000 plus you redo the front walkway and you refresh the bathroom?"

They might accept that, they might not. But you can see how clutter can be useful and you could start throwing in more and more clutter. Even if they accept the walkway redo, you could say, "How about putting in a new hose? I noticed the hose in the back is really old. Can you install a new one?"

Throw some grass seed down; you could even push it after you have an agreed-upon deal. So, clutter is very, very key in negotiating.

In conclusion, both in networking and negotiations you cannot go in with desperation or with dollar signs in your eyes. If people sense that you really, really need this to happen, you will not win the negotiation, and you will not win that networking client or that relationship.

You need to be sincere and, in both cases, you need to be able to walk away. If I were in desperation mode, I would be honest with the other person upfront. This sounds like the opposite of what one should do, but being honest goes a long way; some people might sympathize and do something to at least extend an olive branch to you.

Never, ever lose the leverage in negotiation or making new contacts by having to do it out of desperation unless you are honest about it.

**When you go in there with nothing
to lose, you can only win.**

The next section of the book is really the road to wealth. In the first section of the book we talked a lot about money and mindset. In this section we talked about business, which is really the road to riches.

But ...

In the next section I am going to talk about your pathway to wealth. This would be a good time to take a break, grab a snack and get ready, because once you get started you are not going to want to put the book down.

SECTION 3:

THE ROAD TO WEALTH, INVESTING & REAL ESTATE

Jeff Ramsperger

CHAPTER 9:

INVESTING

An investment in knowledge pays the best interest.
Benjamin Franklin

In Chapter 3, we discussed closing your circle—a vital, spiritual and physical thing that you must do. Unless you know where your money is going, you cannot make more.

I also talked about investing by taking your excess funds and placing them into three different verticals. One of those verticals is savings for a rainy day. Another one is giving, and the third is investing.

In this section I am going to cover the types of investments that are available, and I will give you my opinions on the best vehicles for you and why, plus the spiritual impact of each one.

First, though, I want to cover your spiritual investment. Now, giving is not known as an investment, but for me it has been the best investment I have ever made.

In many faiths, and certainly in the Christian faith, giving is a spiritual act that does get a return. The key to giving is to do so without expecting anything in return. When you give with a cheerful heart, out of your excess, money just comes back to you. In fact, the scriptures call for 10 percent, or a tithe.

This is not a religious act. If you are doing this out of religious responsibility and duty, then please stop, because you are wasting your money. You must give from a heart that knows you are provided for. You are being a good steward with it. When you give 10 percent as a tithe, you are establishing a bank account. I will call it a universal or heavenly bank account. When you tithe, it does not guarantee a return or multiple on your money.

What it does give is a savings account that you can draw from when you need something; it's almost like an insurance policy.

People who tithe tend to have fewer vehicle breakdowns. Maybe the roof on their house will last a little bit longer. It's almost magic how it works. Things that are impossible happen. You get that job you weren't qualified for because the person hiring saw your potential. Just when you need it the most, an unexpected government rebate comes through that covers your need. On a day you are very down a friend comes by with a nice piece of chocolate or your favourite movie.

It is one of these spiritual laws that is undeniable. There have been millions and millions of people who have proved it throughout the centuries. Giving not only makes you feel good and gives back to the world, but there is something I will call the giver's gain formula.

The giver's gain formula is a neat name, but I do not want to contradict my previous words. You do not give to gain. If you do, you will not gain. If you give to have people see you giving, "Oh, look how generous he is at this fundraising dinner, standing up for all to see," I would say you've already received your reward. The recognition of everyone in the room, or people on the street seeing how generous you are, is your reward.

But when you give out of a generous heart, and you are not seeking the attention, then scripture says your money will be multiplied. I have tested this, and it works. Others have tested it too.

My friends Kim and Ross have seen this in action. Many years ago, they felt led to give a gift to a ministry. Even though the amount was relatively small, it might as well have been a million dollars to Kim and Ross, but they gave it anyway.

A few weeks later a sheet of ice came off their roof. It destroyed the front deck of their house and ripped a lot of siding off, but it completely missed the car. The first blessing-protection.

Ross and Kim took pictures with a digital camera, cleaned up the damage but did nothing else because they thought it would be considered an "act of God" and the insurance wouldn't cover it. In the summer of that year, they talked to a friend who convinced them to go to the insurance company and make a claim.

They called the company and a claims adjuster came out. He said he would start a claim but doubted anything would happen because it had been an act of God and the only proof was digital pictures that could have been altered. (Digital photography was new and not widely accepted back then.) Kim and Ross accepted his words and went on with life, hoping at some point to have enough money to fix the house.

About a week later they received a call that their claim had been approved to fix the deck and, not only that, redo the entire roof. Kim and Ross had been having problems with the roof leaking but had no money to fix it. When the ice came down it tore off shingles on each side in a spot that could not be easily fixed, and the whole roof would have to be done.

The reason? The ice had been so bad that year that the government was forcing insurance companies to cover it, and the digital pictures were the proof that it happened.

They had given their gift not expecting anything in return, and they received a thousand-fold back on that investment. Giving does work. Sometimes it's thirty-fold, sometimes it's sixty-fold. Sometimes it's 100 percent. Sometimes you will just be blown away.

TRADITIONAL INVESTMENT STRATEGIES

You do need to invest. If you want to attain wealth or riches, it is the only way. Having a high-paying job might provide a very comfortable living, but you are not multiplying your money and your money is not working for you. You will not achieve your maximum earning potential.

A mortgage broker I have worked with who specializes in working with investors. Dion Beg gave a stunning presentation, and he has given me permission to share some of it in this chapter.

I should mention he is authoring a book right now. I expect that not too long after you read mine, his book will be available. I would suggest searching him out, because he is quite brilliant.

He says there are many different investments out there and a ton of investment vehicles are being offered to you. If you really look at them, they all funnel into three strategies. You can invest in business. You can invest in the market. Or you can invest in real estate.

A lot of choices, isn't it? I can't tell you which one is right for you; only you can decide that. However, I will share some great information from Dion that I hope will point you in the right direction.

Let's say you have $100,000 and you want to invest in business, the market or real estate. You go to your favourite lending institution and say, "Ms. Banker, I have $100,000 and I want to invest in business. I found a turnkey operation with a proven track record, one that is solid; it is a franchise and I am guaranteed to make money. Ms. Banker, I will give you my $100,000. How much will you be able to lend me on my $100,000?"

If you don't need money, I will give you this caveat before we continue any further: the bank will give you as much as you want.

But let's just pretend you need to borrow money and that's the reason you are going to the bank. In this example, with $100,000, you are ready to invest into a turnkey business system. If you were to get $30,000 from the bank, that would have been a successful venture.

Now, let's use the same scenario but look at the market.

"Ms. Banker, I have $100,000 to invest in the market, and I want to use the best guy the bank has. Whatever he says, that's what I am going to do. Ms. Banker, I want to make money in the market. How much money will you loan me to invest?"

Again, I would venture to say that on the $100,000 you have, she will probably offer you about $30,000.

Now, let's look at the third investment strategy, real estate.

"Ms. Banker, I have $100,000 to invest in real estate. I found a great house, and I am making a little bit of money in the buy. How much money will you give me?" Ms. Banker says, "I will give you $400,000."

Now, the bank has a lot of money. They've done very well in using your money to create profit. Banks don't like to lose. Which investment vehicle is the bank telling you is the best one to take in this scenario?

Let's look at the spiritual aspects of these three investment vehicles.

Remember back at the beginning of this book, where we discussed money and the spirit of money and how it was managed before currency was created. It took the form of land, houses, livestock, again which was a business strategy; gold, which I relate to current times as being your assets; and silver, which is your working capital.

Going back to the original and remember this has not changed. Same God, same universe yesterday as today.

God believes in business. I believe that business is a great vehicle for you to invest in if you have a proper business plan, have done your market research and know who your target audience is. You must be capitalized well enough.

Too many businesses fail because they don't go in with enough money to run the business. You have to be realistic, and if you're not an experienced business person, you need to seek out counsel or a mentor —

someone who has done it before in the business you are looking at. If you are trying to reinvent the wheel, don't do it. Find somebody; it will save you a ton of money and heartache.

Business is what I will call a Creator investment strategy.

Let's look at the market from the spiritual aspect.

The market is man's invention to raise capital to help businesses expand. The market is similar, in my estimation, to the invention of currency, which, as you will remember from Chapter 3, changed all of the rules.

I will ask you this question: is man both good and evil? Can Mammon play in this space with ease? I would say the answer to both of those questions is yes.

Now, it is true that the market creates a lot of wealth, and I have some friends who do very well in the market every day. They are generating huge profits. They know what they are doing, and they use excess money. It is not their main wealth-creation strategy. If they lose their portfolio in the market overnight, they are still okay.

My humble opinion on the subject is that if you want to play in the market, that's great. Find someone who is an expert and proceed but invest your excess only.

So, the market is created as opposed to business, which is from the Creator.

Now, let's look at real estate. I would put real estate in the same category as business. It is from the Creator. It is fairly common knowledge that 90 percent of millionaires today achieved at least a portion of their wealth through real estate. Business is usually a part of the portfolio, but almost every successful businessman also invests in real estate. In real estate, if you are educated in proper investing, it is very hard to lose.

When I started investing in real estate, I looked at the trend lines for the last seventy years. There were some dips, but it always recovers, and the prices keep going up.

I will give you more specifics on real estate investing in the next chapter. But out of those three options, I hope this example has given you some insight into the ways you will want to invest your excess money.

Now, let's look at investments from a 30,000-foot view and see what your earning potential is.

I love basic math, and I love when numbers show you results. Numbers don't lie. Numbers can be manipulated, but if you are wise and in business or in real estate or in the market, if you watch the numbers you can do very well.

THE RULE OF 72 AND THE DOUBLING GAME

In this section I want to illustrate the power of investment. I am going to combine two very basic things that will show you how to determine your risk tolerance. Any time you invest in those three strategies, there is risk. It will also help illustrate your potential earnings. If you use it correctly, you can also work backward from your age.

For instance, if you are thirty years old, you might say, "I have thirty years to invest and then I want to sit back at sixty and live off my investments." If you are sixty years old, you might say, "You know, I have never invested in my life. I am in good health and I can invest for the next ten years. What could I make based on this?"

Here's how the rule of 72 and the doubling game works: let's first look at the rule of 72.

Definition: the rule of 72 is a simplified way to determine how long an investment will take to double given a fixed annual rate of interest.

It's about doubling your money. As an example, if you were to make a 10 percent return on your money, using the rule of 72 it will take you 7.2 years to double your money. Not bad, right?

What type of return should you get for what you are getting currently?

Let's look at this first. If you have your money in a savings account, you're making 1.0 to 1.5 percent interest. Minus bank fees, teller fees, transaction fees. You might be losing. So, keeping your money in a savings account is probably not a great idea.

> *"How many millionaires do you know who have become wealthy by investing in savings accounts? I rest my case."*
> *Robert G. Allen*

If you have a self-directed or a managed plan, like a mutual fund or something like that, an 8-percent return on your money is very common. It's not bad; it's better than not investing. But, again, when you take away commissions and transaction fees, that 8 percent, when it's managed by someone else, usually comes out to about a 5-percent return on your money. At 5 percent it's going to take you 14.4 years to double your money using the rule of 72.

Now, 15 percent is a really great return and it's very possible. In fact, for purposes of this exercise, I will use 15 percent, but be aware 20 percent is very possible. Even 30 and 40 percent and higher return per year on your money is very possible.

Now that I've described the rule of 72, let's look at the doubling game.

The rule of 72 tells you how long it will take to double your money at a certain interest rate, but let's look at doubling alone.

If you were to start with $1,000, how many times would you have to double your money to get to a million dollars? The answer is ten.

$1,000 ➤ $2,000 ➤ $4,000 ➤$8,000 ➤ $16,000 ➤ $32,000 ➤ $64,000 ➤ $128,000 ➤ $256,000 ➤ $512,000 ➤ $1,024,000.

We would all love to double our money. How do you do it?

One thing I have done in the past is go to websites where people sell stuff. If you know what you are doing, you can buy something, make money in the buy—they just want to get rid of it—then sell it and double your money. I have done this so many times, sometimes just for fun.

At one point I wanted to start camping again. So, I bought a camping trailer for my motorcycle for about half of what it was worth and brought it home. My wife wasn't very enthusiastic about it, and when I looked at the trailer I thought, "You know, I really don't want to put a trailer hitch on my motorcycle." So, I put it for sale. I more than doubled my money on that thing in a week.

Let's look at this in the second way, and that is real estate. In real estate, 15 percent is easily achievable. In

Canada you have to make a 20-percent down payment on an investment property. So, for 20 percent on a $300,000 house, which is a good price for a house both in the United States and in Canada as an investment property, I would require $60,000.

With a $60,000 investment, in 4.8 years I will have doubled my money and have $120,000. Continuing with 15 percent in 9.6 years, that $60,000 will have turned into $240,000. In 14.4 years, it will be $480,000. In 19.2 years, it will be $960,000. In 24 years, that $60,000 investment will be $1,920,000.

If you are thirty years old and you are reading this book right now, pay attention. If you are forty years old, pay attention. If you are sixty years old— well, $60,000 into $240,000. Would that help your retirement? I would think so.

Now, the beauty of this, not only in real estate but in business, is that as your assets increase in value, you can pull out your original investment, and maybe some additional money from that business or property and start another doubling-game vertical.

Let's take that $60,000 investment after 4.8 years, when it's worth $120,000. Let's say you could pull $60,000 or $80,000 out of that and start doubling your money again while your first doubling-money cycle continues.

Now you are not only doubling, you are quadrupling your money. You do this over and over and over. It is absolutely amazing. I will cover details on how this works in the next chapter. If you are an uneducated investor and you just go and buy an investment property, you may get lucky and see these returns,

Jeff Ramsperger

but you really have to be educated to understand how to create these returns.

WHY SHOULD YOU PAY OFF YOUR HOUSE FAST?

This is a very interesting question. If you have a very low risk tolerance, paying your house off fast is a good idea. In fact, with standard mortgage rules if you take a twenty-five-year mortgage and you pay bi-weekly instead of monthly, you will take about seven years off and save yourself a lot of money in interest payments.

Why do you want to pay the bank for the privilege of borrowing the money? However, is your house really an asset that makes you money? If you take an eighteen- or twenty-five- or even thirty-year mortgage, your house will appreciate in that time. If you buy the house for $300,000 and in ten years it's worth $600,000, most people say, "I made $300,000 on my house." But if you look at how much you actually paid for that house, including your interest payments, and the other fees associated with owning a house, i.e., property taxes, was it really a good investment?

I like to look at it this way: if your house is making you money after doing the calculations for yourself, then it is a good investment. If your house isn't making you money, it is not a good investment. If your house is not making you money, most people who get into real estate investing, or even for business, will borrow against their house.

So, if you have an interest rate on your house of let's say 2.7 percent—the interest rate you are paying

120

the bank — and you could borrow at 3.5 percent using a line of credit against your house, and you use that borrowed money to get a higher rate of return on another investment product, now your house has become an asset and starts making you money.

Again, if you were to borrow at 3.5 percent, and you were to make that 15 percent, you are making 11.5 percent using someone else's money. You are using the bank's money to do it.

Now your house has become a money maker. By the way, if you invest it in a business that turns profitable or you invest in real estate, when that asset starts to appreciate you can pull your money out again and start another vertical to double your money.

In the next chapter, we are going to get into a lot more detail on real estate. It's only one chapter, so it will not teach you to become an expert on real estate investing, but I will paint a clear picture for you of different strategies and maybe give you an idea of what you should invest your time and getting educated in.

If you are excited about how much money you can make using the rule of 72 and the doubling game, you are going to love this next chapter

Jeff Ramsperger

CHAPTER 10:

REAL ESTATE

"Buy land, they're not making it anymore."

Mark Twain

Why does real estate create wealth?

In the previous chapter I talked about how you could borrow money against real estate investments and how much more ability you have in real estate to borrow than in the other two strategies, which are business and the market.

In this chapter, I want to give you additional information on investing in real estate and how it will work for you. This is the game 90 percent of millionaires have used as a vehicle of wealth creation. It is hard to lose money in real estate. To lose money in real estate, you either have to make a very high-risk move or simply be uneducated on how to buy in real estate and how to make the numbers work.

Many people who invest in real estate just think, *I know the neighbourhood, and I know that house is a nice house; my house went up in value.* So, a house comes up for sale and they buy another house, a single-family home.

First of all, I don't call that decision real estate investing, because it's an uneducated investment. Sure, we've all been told that you are an expert just by knowing location, location, location. Well-educated real estate investors do look at the location, but it's not the single determining factor for buying a home.

When buying a home as an investment, I would rarely recommend buying a single-family home. If you buy a single-family home and your renter moves out or you get stuck with a bad renter who doesn't pay their bills, you have nothing coming in and that house costs you money.

It is better to have a duplex, a triplex, a four-plex or something more, because it minimizes your risk. In my seminars I get into deeper detail on this. If you would like to find out more about my seminars, go to: www.affinitytoaffluence.com.

It's important to say an educated investor does not just use location as a main factor. In fact, when someone says they buy because of location, what they are really saying is they are buying for appreciation, meaning the value of the house goes up consistently.

The savvy real estate investor loves appreciation when it comes but in truth buys for cash flow. Cash flow in real estate investing means *after* paying all your bills, and after delegating property management, because do you really want to deal with landlord/tenant issues? Probably not. So, after building that into your budget, after building in the cost of annual repairs, after building in improvements to your building ... Put all that into your spreadsheet to see if there is positive cash flow per door or per unit.

That is the way an investor looks at it. When people attend my seminars or buy some of my additional products, I do provide our spreadsheets. They are pre-formulated, and if you follow them you'll know if it's a good investment or a bad investment seconds after populating the spreadsheets.

I am going to give you a really quick formula for looking at investment properties. I call it my ten-second formula.

Looking at a hundred properties (not in person, just online) takes time. But when you visit the book website www.affinitytoaffluence.com you get my ten-second formula, which enables you to assess a property, as long as you have a little bit of background information on the location and what you are looking at. Within ten seconds you can determine whether you want to spend more time looking at it or not. Go and get your free download right now.

I cannot stress this enough. Don't just go out and start buying investment properties. Invest in your training first. I know you may be excited to get going, but if you truly want to make money, education is the best investment in you.

RISK FACTORS

In the previous chapter when we talked about the return on investment and the doubling game, you got a snapshot of how long it would take you to get a certain amount of money.

Now, if you have a goal and you want to retire with a certain amount of money, your risk factors are determined by the amount of return you need on your investment per annum. That's why I put together the rule of 72 and the doubling game. This will help you determine your risk factor.

With any real estate investment there is risk, although for the most part it is safe in the long term. There is always risk potential. Let's look at the three different types of real estate strategies I use and the risk involved.

The first one to look at is a **low-risk rent-to-own strategy.** Rent-to-own helps people who are unable to qualify for a mortgage but want to get into their own home. Rent-to-own in my opinion is a very-low-risk strategy to build wealth.

Rent-to-own has had a bit of a tarnished reputation. Although it is a brilliant strategy that can really help people, the unfortunate part is if the rent-to-own tenant does not fulfill their obligations, they lose, and the investor makes a lot of money.

Remember, not all people are good people, and some investors have bought in the past, and probably do even today, with the aim of filling their rent-to-own properties with tenants who will never make it. They are essentially robbing them.

This goes against my ethics; I will not enter into this. In fact, I will make every effort to help my rent-to-own clients succeed, even if I make less money.

Now the client is typically someone who has damaged credit or just does not qualify for a mortgage. In Canada, particularly right now, this is related to a stress test. Even though you are going to borrow at 2.6 percent, your payments are calculated using 5 percent interest to see if you will be able to pay for it, if the interest rates went increase.

So, if you have previously qualified for a house at $400,000, you will probably only qualify, using the stress test in Canada, for about $300,000, which takes away a lot of your buying power. This is why young professionals, even though they make good money, often cannot qualify for the mortgage they want. Rent-to-own also helps people who are new to the country, people who don't have an established credit but have money and have established themselves in a job. They make money and will share the house with family to ease the financial burden. These are great candidates for rent-to-own.

My real estate investment company will typically find a person who qualifies for rent-to-own. Obviously, the person has to be interested and want to get into their own house. Perhaps they even want to have a pet, which is not as easy with some rentals in some markets. Many landlords do not allow pets. You can really, really help people experience that pride of ownership, getting into their own house and having their kids consistently going to a school, through rent-to-own.

When I am scrutinizing applicants for rent-to-own, I make them go to our mortgage broker. The mortgage broker gives assurances that there is a pathway for this person to take over ownership of the house in two to three years. Most rent-to-own deals are three years, some are two; some you may have to extend to four for the person to take over the house. That is usually negotiated upfront or afterward.

With rent-to-own, the applicant must have a down payment. If someone does not have a down payment, they do not qualify. That's the first disqualifier for a rent-to-own candidate. I typically want 3 to 4 percent of the purchase price of the home I will be purchasing on their behalf.

Let's say on a $300,000 home, the client gives me $12,000 (4 percent) as a down payment. That down payment is my security. I will use it to help them purchase the house later on, so I keep that money, but it's really their money. If something happens and they do not make it to the end of the contract, I have the right to that money. But if they fulfill their end, that money is used toward their down payment.

If someone does not have a down payment, they are never going to be a homeowner. If they cannot save up money to start, they are not going to get there.

After they qualify, I send them out with our real estate agent in the area that is chosen. We typically give them four to ten houses to look at that fit the criteria. We do not let them look at twenty or thirty properties. They are most likely not going to get their dream house; they are going to get a good house in a good area. They cannot go over the budget we have set for them. Let's say, for example, the real estate agent shows them a $350,000 home. He must be 100-percent confident that he can get it for $300,000 or we fire him. He is off our team immediately because he violated our parameters.

If the rent-to-own client cannot qualify for a house that costs more than the amount we determined, we are taking away their pathway. We are being unethical, and so is the agent. So, we put out these very strict guidelines for real estate agents.

The house is then selected, and we buy it. We've already received our client's money and our contracts are very specific. Now, I will tell you that in our rent-to-own portfolio we typically average 29-percent ROI year after year. You need to be educated to be able to get those returns.

If the market-value rent on a rent-to-own house is $1,600 per month, the rent-to-own tenant will pay the $1,600 per month—market value—plus they will cover the utilities and any basic repairs under $500. This is how I structure my deals.

In addition to paying the $1,600, they will make what we call an option-consideration payment. Essentially, we put them into a forced savings plan that will increase their down payment when combined with their original down payment. So, if we added an optional-payment-for-savings plan of $400 per month over a term of three years, that's another $14,400 that the rent-to-own client has accumulated.

In my seminars I give very specific information on how to do this and how to work the cash flow. There are some great things about rent-to-own: you can actually get very good cash flow out of this strategy and be safe and make a pretty good return on your money.

Now, here's the magic. The house will most likely appreciate, because you have done your due diligence on the area and the market is good. So, let's assume the house goes up five percent per year for three years. What we do is split the appreciation with the tenant. We make some money off of this, but we also leave some skin in the game for the client.

Now think of someone who has never owned a house before. If they have saved up the $20,000 and have never missed a payment, and they have saved up that additional $14,400 in their optional consideration, they have $34,400, plus we are giving them some of the appreciation of the house. If the house has gone up $40,000, we split it with them and they get $20,000 more. Now they've got a really good start. They have equity in the home they are buying that they can use, and it helps them qualify for the mortgage. They win; we win. It's a great scenario.

A medium-risk real estate strategy is the most popular one available. It's called buy, rent and hold. In other words, you buy the property, you rent it out, and you hold onto it. I call this a medium-risk real estate strategy but only if it's short term. If you buy long term and you are an educated investor, I would say this is also a very safe low-risk investment strategy.

This is the strategy where feel you can make the most money. Long term," to "I feel you can make the most money, long term, and it's one I highly recommend.

Rent-to-own is a great strategy, very safe, and you feel good doing it, and it's a way of giving back to society and helping people up, but I suggest, if you are getting into real estate, that buy, rent and hold is probably the best one for most of the portfolio you are going to create.

As mentioned in the introduction to this chapter, buy, rent and hold in my opinion should not be used for a single-family home. There may be exceptions to the rule, but buying a duplex, triplex or something bigger will minimize your risk with vacant apartments if you have problematic tenants, and it gives you a wonderful opportunity to make more money.

There are many ways you can make money with the buy, rent and hold property. One of them is what I call forced appreciation. Let's say you were to buy a four-plex property, and you made a little bit of money in the buy. One of the great strategies is realized when the previous owner, whom you are buying it from, will help you with the down payment. This is not uncommon when you get into multi-dwelling residences. In my training courses, I teach strategies where you can even go into these without using any of your own money at all.

If you go in with zero money, any return you get is infinite. However, let's say you use your own money, which is common; you can increase the value of the property in many different ways.

If you improve the building, you improve the value of the building. Also, raising rents. Even if it's a very small percentage every year, over time it adds up, and the amount of revenue the building is generating, increases its value.

Putting in coin-laundry systems can add value. Perhaps there is a garage you can rent out separately to either your tenants or to someone else. This, again, increases the value of your property. When you increase the value of your property it appreciates—it's worth more when you sell it. Even more importantly, it's worth more when you take your money out and use it again.

Remember how we talked about having multiple verticals in the rule of 72 and the doubling game? Let's say you went into this property with $100,000, and after a couple of years, you can take your money out of the property, refinance and buy another property with it. How much more are you making with two properties than with just one?

Now, very importantly with buy, rent and hold: you must cover all your expenses. You should build in property management, you should build in being able to appreciate your property. You build annual maintenance, and a rainy-day fund, into your spreadsheets. You need to make cash flow per door—positive cash flow, unless you are wealthy, and you don't care.

Some investors are happy with $50 per door. Depending on the size of the building and the number of doors, that might be good. If it is a smaller building, $100 per door positive cash flow might be good. You might be able to get a lot more than that.

Again, get educated and get onboard. Get educated and make good decisions.

The last real estate investment strategy I want to cover in this chapter is **flipping, and it has the highest risk.** This is on TV everywhere. If it's on TV, it must be the greatest thing to do. Flipping houses is a great business.

Even if you know what you are doing, I am going to put this in the high-risk category. Unfortunately, because it's on TV, and so prevalent in our culture because of TV, everyone thinks they can do it, and a lot of people are getting hurt.

If you are going to get into flipping, you must calculate before you buy a worst-case strategy. In fact, with any of these strategies I'm laying out, an educated investor has an exit plan—an Option B and an Option C in case option A does not work out.

Option B and Option C allow you to escape without you losing money. If you cannot come up with those options, don't do it. That would be my advice.

Flipping houses is high-risk. If you can plan for the worst-case scenario, if you have trustworthy skilled trades, if you have a great team around you that can get in and get out, and if you are confident that the market is hot enough that you can turn the house over in a short period of time, it is a great way to generate cash.

I am not against flipping. I have done a flip myself. I will do more flips in the future. It's just not my focus.

ONE LAST PIECE OF ADVICE

Here's how I look at real estate investing: there are many strategies. In fact, there are several more strategies that I haven't listed here. But those I have shared in some detail in this chapter are very popular and very good strategies.

What it comes down to for me is finding the right property. There are entire books dedicated to this, so I'm not even going to attempt to cover it now.

Here's the essence of it: find a property you can make money on in the buy. If you can make money in the buy, then you have a good property to work with. You can wholesale the property, which means giving it to someone else. "Look, I found a property that you can make money on in the buy," and they will pay you for finding the deal.

But if you can make money in the buy, then you can look at the property and determine the best strategy for that property. I don't specifically look for buy, rent and hold houses, and I certainly don't specifically look for rent-to-own unless I have a rent-to-own client who is ready to move in.

I look for properties where I can make money in the buy and then, because I am an educated investor, I decide on the best thing to do with that property.

Want to apply to invest with me? Visit www. vipscorp.ca

I have given you some great tools to learn how to make money in business or in real estate, even if you are an employee, or you are starting a business. I trust you will be highly successful because of reading this book.

The next chapter is more about living in your success, and it's a fun chapter—one that you wouldn't expect from reading the content of these ten chapters. I am super excited to introduce the next chapter to you.

Don't put the book down now. Keep reading. It's super fun, and you are going to enjoy it immensely.

CHAPTER 11:

LISTEN TO THE MUSIC

Wealth consists not in having great possessions but having few wants.

Epictetus

What an adventure we have been on. I hope that reading this book has encouraged you as much as I have enjoyed writing it. What a joy to share with you what I have learned about becoming affluent and living a great life. I am honoured you have joined me on this journey, and now it is coming to an end. Let's take a quick look at what we have learned so far.

You have a choice in life, and you can choose to be rich or even wealthy. You are not trapped by your circumstances; you can become more if you decide to give up complacency. You will have to change a bit, especially your mindset, if you want your life to be different.

Money has two sides to it: the physical and the spiritual. The two must be in agreement if you want wealth to come to you. The advanced law of attraction is an important part of your road to wealth. You need to not only understand it but use it to your advantage.

You must put actions to your beliefs. Money will not fall out of the sky. You have to earn it, and I covered three ways to do this: through business, investing and real estate. The more of these actions you take, the wealthier you become.

Now comes one of my favourite parts: teaching you how to enjoy the wealth you have earned. There are wealthy people who are miserable, who never spend a single penny and die unhappy and regretful. Don't be that person! Learn to listen to the music.

I want to share with you some of the lessons I have learned that have helped me enjoy the moments of life and truly appreciate the blessings in my life.

THE MUSIC IS YOURS

Listen to the Music is not just a great song by the Doobie Brothers. It is a metaphor for the way I look at life. Music is the photo album of my life, and I bet it has been for you as well. Have you ever heard a song that takes you back to a great memory? Songs are associated with some of the most beautiful moments of my life.

This title is also a metaphor for simply having an appreciation of the beauty we experience every day, whether it is the beauty in other people or the astounding beauty of nature that surrounds us.

In this book I have talked a lot about the importance of being thankful and how it opens up doors and presents opportunities that are aligned with your passions. When opportunities present themselves and you embrace them, life becomes more fantastic, more beautiful, and you become more appreciative.

An important note about this book and the system of wealth creation that I have built for you: if you plan to use the tools I've written about here, you have to start living as if it is a reality already.

When you buy something, don't look for the cheapest price every time. Instead, look for the best quality and value that is within your budget. I would say that if you cannot get what you want right away, it is wise to continue saving and growing your funds until you can get the things you really want and deserve.

Oftentimes when you try to save money on something it ends up costing them more. Eventually, when the thing they saved money on ends up in the trash, either for lack of quality or dissatisfaction with the product or service, you spend the money again, hopefully having learned the lesson.

For me a key example of this is with audio systems. I have worked intimately with audio all my life and it is a huge passion for me. Too often I see someone who is buying a new stereo or set of speakers spend a fraction of what they should spend, and the result is embarrassing. Yet people will spend a ton of money on a supersize TV that, isn't the best quality. They missed that having a great audio system truly lets you appreciate what the artist intended you to hear.

Why do you need that TV anyway? The truly wealthy have big libraries, not big TVs. They use their time wisely and learn. I am not saying you should not have a TV—just don't live your life through it.

If you do not start living like you have money, you most likely will not achieve your financial goals, because you don't believe in them. I am not saying to live life recklessly or foolishly, but you must get rid of a poverty attitude. I like to buy quality products when they are on sale, but I'm not going to cut coupons and drive ten miles and spend an extra half an hour to save five dollars. That is an example of a poverty attitude. My time is worth way more than the five dollars I saved.

As mentioned in the networking section of this book, splurging a little bit—taking that better vacation, for example—also positions you to seize better opportunities. Everyone has their own passions and desires. I am simply saying that when you are buying or experiencing those things that are aligned with your passions and desires, go the extra step and make sure you do it right. It is wonderful what happens not only in your physical surroundings but in your spiritual environment as well.

Another very useful tool is paying it forward. This works hand in hand with giving and not expecting anything back. When you pay it forward, you spread joy and you invite more joy into your life. The result is that you are trusted with more, and more is given.

One thing that is of the utmost importance to me is leaving a legacy. Generating wealth in my life and in my relationships, particularly with God, is supposed to be generational. I not only desire to pass along material things of beauty and to provide to the best of my ability for future generations in my family and other relationships, but I want to make a mark on this world. Yes, it is true: I believe that every person in this world makes a difference. I want the difference that I create to be substantial. I want to pass on my heart. What I mean by that is I want to teach people the dignity of hard work, appreciation, and love of thy neighbour.

Most of my clients are either in the middle class or upper middle class financially speaking. My heart really has a spot for people in this category. When I mentioned in The Five Hollywood Scripts the term reactionaryism, I felt some sorrow around that sentiment. That complacency trap is deceptive. You think you are staying still, but in reality, you are moving backward and don't know it until it is too late.

The economies in most of the western civilization are designed to keep commoners in this place. It encourages spending, wastefulness and debt, keeping people trapped for the rest of their lives. Please don't be that person. You can escape that trap and live your desired life.

YOUR FIRST STEPS

Now that you have finished this book, I want you to go through it again—this time slower. There are nuggets throughout that you need to read again and think about. Highlight them and meditate on how they can be applied to your life. These are called "Aha!" moments, and they are the ones that change your life.

The second step is to assess where you are right now. Be honest with yourself. The only way you will ever become more is if you can see yourself as you truly are with both strengths and weaknesses.

The third step: Dare to dream. This may be the most powerful exercise in the book. Write down a list of desires, things your heart longs for. It may be a relationship, material things, a new employment opportunity, business, etc. Here is what you do with this list: look at it three times daily—morning, noon and night. Read the list slowly enough to hear the words in your head, and then take a moment to meditate on the list. You will be amazed how things start to show up or pathways appear that go toward your desires.

Step four is to learn. There are many skills you will need to learn to create wealth. Take a short period of time to learn what you need to do first to move forward. I would suggest not taking a long time, as it is easy to get into analysis paralysis and never do anything.

Step five is to start taking action. Yes, this will involve risk, but anything worth doing is worth some risk. Work with what you have. Start surrounding yourself with the people who are going in the direction you want to go. Your net worth depends on it!

If you have enjoyed this book, then I encourage you to connect with me for more training. I love coaching people from where they are to a fulfilled, wealthy, happy life. I have lots of resources available to help you, and my greatest joy would be to see you at one of my training seminars or events.

Visit www.thespeakerscompany.com

As this book has now come to conclusion, I want to leave you with one last quote.

"Truly I tell you, if anyone says to this mountain, 'Go, throw yourself into the sea,' and does not doubt in their heart but believes that what they say will happen, it will be done for them. Therefore, I tell you, whatever you ask for in prayer, believe that you have received it, and it will be yours."

Jesus

Live Your Desired Life ™
Jeff Ramsperger

Jeff Ramsperger

ABOUT AUTHOR

Jeff's first forays into entrepreneurship as a child only fueled what would become his life-long passion. Business.

With over 30 years experience Jeff has done it all. From teacher to public speaker to mentor to coach to consultant and real estate investor. One of Jeff's biggest loves has always been audio/video where he has worked with some of the largest brands in the world.

Jeff is always achieving record-setting growth by implementing a passion-for-people approach and understanding the needs and wants of his clients. As a public speaker, author, mentor and coach, Jeff has dedicated his life to helping you to Live your Desired Life™. Jeff teaches you the most direct path to creating riches and wealth by operating in your passion and following the rules and Spirit of Money.

In real estate Jeff has become very successful owning many properties and especially enjoys helping those who don't qualify through traditional methods to become home owners, through his rent-to-own program.

If you are interested in having Jeff speak, train or emcee at your event go to www.thespeakerscompany. com